Narrative Therapy for Women Experiencing Domestic Violence

of related interest

Rebuilding Lives after Domestic Violence
Understanding Long-Term Outcomes
Hilary Abrahams
ISBN 978 1 84310 961 7

Supporting Women after Domestic Violence
Loss, Trauma and Recovery
Hilary Abrahams
Foreword by Cathy Humphreys
ISBN 978 1 84310 431 5

Counselling Survivors of Domestic Abuse
Christiane Sanderson
ISBN 978 1 84310 606 7

Picking up the Pieces After Domestic Violence
A Practical Resource for Supporting Parenting Skills
Kate Iwi and Chris Newman
ISBN 978 1 84905 021 0

Domestic Violence and Child Protection
Directions for Good Practice
Edited by Cathy Humphreys and Nicky Stanley
ISBN 978 1 84310 276 2

Mothering Through Domestic Violence
Lorraine Radford and Marianne Hester
ISBN 978 1 84310 473 5

Making an Impact – Children and Domestic Violence
A Reader
2nd edition
Marianne Hester, Chris Pearson and Nicola Harwin
With Hilary Abrahams
ISBN 978 1 84310 157-4

Violence Against Women in South Asian Communities
Issues for Policy and Practice
Edited by Ravi K Thiara and Aisha K Gill
Foreword by Professor Liz Kelly CBE
ISBN 978 1 84310 670 8

Narrative Therapy for Women Experiencing Domestic Violence

Supporting Women's Transitions from Abuse to Safety

Mary Allen

Foreword by Ravi K. Thiara

Jessica Kingsley *Publishers*
London and Philadelphia

First published in 2012
by Jessica Kingsley Publishers
116 Pentonville Road
London N1 9JB, UK
and
400 Market Street, Suite 400
Philadelphia, PA 19106, USA

www.jkp.com

Library of Congress Cataloging in Publication Data
Allen, Mary.
Narrative therapy for women experiencing domestic violence : supporting women's transitions from abuse to safety / Mary Allen.
p. cm.
Includes bibliographical references and index.
ISBN 978-1-84905-190-3 (alk. paper)
1. Family violence. 2. Abused women. 3. Women--Violence against--Prevention. 4. Women--Violence against--Treatment. 5. Narrative therapy. I. Title.
HV6626.A424 2012
616.85'8220651--dc23
2011026731

British Library Cataloguing in Publication Data
A CIP catalogue record for this book is available from the British Library

ISBN 978 1 84905 190 3
eISBN 978 0 85700 420 8

Printed and bound in Great Britain

Contents

Foreword

Domestic abuse not only inflicts physical injury on women but leaves enduring emotional and psychological scars which erode women's sense of self, esteem and identity. Emotional abuse is frequently described by women as harder to deal with and recover from because of its on-going effects, something which can take women many years if they are not provided with appropriate support. Despite the deeply damaging impact of domestic abuse, however, women show admirable strength and resilience which eventually leads to their exit from abusive situations. Indeed, women resist in numerous ways, as elaborated in this book, and their strategies often evolve in response to the changing nature of abuse.

The interiority of domestic abuse – secrecy and isolation – has been amply highlighted by research which foregrounds women's narratives. However, these insights are not always utilised in the professional interventions which women encounter when they perform the final act of resistance to abuse, that of leaving abusive partners. Starting new lives and carving out new 'selves' is amongst the most challenging of experiences for women who have lived with abusive men who exercise high levels of control over them, something for which they need the support and expertise of sensitive and insightful 'helpers'. The provision of practical and emotional support to help women in 'moving on' and re-building their lives has been central to the work of domestic violence services and the aim of the women's movement to end violence against women. Currently, the emphasis on practical help – finding new homes and securing incomes – has at times taken second place to longer term therapeutic support, itself complex because of the legacy of coercive control.

The move from victim to survivor is not a linear progression but, as graphically illustrated in this book, a complex, contradictory and fluid process, requiring great negotiation, reconstruction and reconfiguration on the part of a woman. Women's journeys out of abusive situations to rebuilding their lives are complex, not least because they shift the power away from the abuser to the woman. Race/ethnicity, disability, class and age all add extra dimensions to women's experiences; and professional responses can be crucial for women's journeys. As well as providing important insight into women's journeys and responses, this book signals a way, through narrative approaches, for professionals to intervene and offer support that are premised on women re-authoring their biographies. Indeed, the lens of lived experience can help us to make sense of a situation. Narrative approaches have increasingly been used in helping to make sense of and create new ways of describing issues or problem relationships. Unlike traditional therapeutic approaches which pathologies abused women as passive 'victims', the narrative approach outlined in this book avails a view of women as survivors, which foregrounds women's resistance through a reframing of their apparent passivity/helplessness and lack of agency, who find numerous and creative ways to resist. Instead of 'fixing' women in their 'victimhood', understanding women's responses to their abusive situations provides a picture of women as constantly changing and re-negotiating their identities in response to their abuse experiences. Experiences of abuse leave women forever changed, something that creates the need for them to re-formulate their identities in ways that affirm self-hood once they have performed the ultimate 'act of resistance', leaving the abusive relationship. The challenge for professional intervention is how questions can be asked which enable women to recognise their own skilled resistance behaviours to their abuse.

Through the central use of women's narratives, complex concepts are brought to life in this book, which aims to inform social work, counselling and other professional practice to be better informed by women's individual experiences of domestic abuse and the meaning given by women to such experiences. By tracing women's journeys through the abuse, it seeks to offer insights into the ways in which women search for meaning, survival and a redefinition of their 'selves'. Experience has been at the heart of a feminist epistemology and, indeed, to the development of interventions by the movement to end violence against women. For years now, the willingness and engagement of women has enabled researchers to provide greater insights into the lives of women who live with, resist and finally leave domestic abuse. Through their voices, women have enabled improved professional responses to better ensure safety for women and children. Hearing and representing women's voices is also, importantly, at the heart of this book. Just as a feminist methodology foregrounds experience as a route to liberating knowledge, narrative approaches reflect this in practice by emphasising the centrality of women's subjectivity. Keeping women's voices at its heart, and through its focus on identity, meaning and resistance in women's journeys out of abuse, the author develops a narrative intervention approach which can be used by professionals working with abused women. By listening to the meanings women construct for their responses to abuse, and taking cognisance of their various strategies of resistance, professional interventions can thus emanate and be potentially liberating for women.

The struggle against violence against women is by no means over. The dedication of women and others has helped to bring it out of its secretive silence into the public domain so that more conversations can take place. The enduring problem of domestic abuse reveals the nooks and crannies of gendered inequality, something that remains a focus of struggle throughout the world. In particular, post-separation safety and support remain crucial for women's on-going recovery, something that is not always recognised by the crisis intervention nature of services encouraged by current funding regimes. This book is a timely and powerful reminder of the importance of considering women's post-separation recovery and the accompanying support, and funding, necessary to facilitate this.

For women to reclaim and reconstruct themselves through giving their own meaning to their experiences of abuse and resistance is a powerful and transformative process and which can be facilitated by professionals with the necessary insight into women's complex journeys. This book, at a time when domestic violence is increasingly 'professionalised', provides greater insight into women's constant reconstruction of meaning about their experiences. Given that the danger of professionals disempowering women further is ever present, and by drawing on research in the fields of domestic violence and therapeutic approaches, the book suggests a transformative model for professional intervention – a Narrative Intervention for Intimate Partner Violence - which takes cognisance of women's experiences and meaning about their complex journeys from abuse to safety whilst retaining the link to wider social, cultural and gender discourses. It provides an important new way to conceptualise women's journeys through the subjective and complex interrelationship between self-identity, meaning reconstruction and resistance. The approach keeps women's voices and concerns at its heart and suggests questions that professionals can ask. It advocates a model which, if embraced, has the potential to make professional intervention not only more effective but also more efficient.

Ravi K. Thiara
Principal Research Fellow
Centre for the Study of Safety and Well-being
University of Warwick, UK

Chapter 1

Introduction

> One day, a few days after the liberation, I walked through the country past flowering meadows, for miles and miles, toward the market town near the camp. Larks rose to the sky and I could hear their joyous song. There was no one to be seen for miles around; there was nothing but the wide earth and sky and larks' jubilation and the freedom of space. I stopped, looked around, and up to the sky – and then I went down on my knees. At that moment there was little I knew of myself or of the world – I had but one sentence in mind – always the same: 'I called to the Lord from my narrow prison and He answered me in the freedom of space.' How long I knelt there and repeated this sentence memory can no longer recall. *But I know that on that day, in that hour, my new life started.* Step for step I progressed, until I became a human being.
>
> *Victor Frankl (1962, pp.89–90)*

There are clear parallels between the experiences of the women who leave abusive relationships and the reflections of Victor Frankl, quoted above, on his liberation from Auschwitz at the end of the Second World War. The second last sentence has been italicised in the extract quoted above, as it captures so precisely the experiences of many women who have been released from control and lethal threats to their safety, wellbeing and psychological integrity. It is appropriate to begin this text on women's experiences of leaving abusive relationships with Frankl's reflections on his liberation as he used the horror of his internment in Auschwitz to inform his therapeutic practice and the elaboration of logotherapy, which focuses on the 'meaning of human existence' and the individual's 'search for such a meaning' (Frankl 1962, p.99).

It is the purpose of this book to enable the experiences of women who have survived domestic abuse, and the meaning of these experiences for these women, to inform social work, counselling and other professional practice theory. In order to do this it will listen to the voices of these women as they articulate their narratives of, and reflections on, their individual experiences. It will reflect on and discuss the concepts of identity, resistance and meaning making in these journeys, as they too seek and achieve safety and a 'new life'. These theoretical concepts will be elucidated in detail in later chapters as they have emerged within a range of professional and research literature. Narrative Therapy provides an appropriate counselling method to facilitate this exploration and support, and this book outlines the use of Narrative Intervention for Intimate Partner Violence.

Before a 'new life' can be achieved however, another life must be experienced, survived and overcome. Throughout this book, the contours, dangers and resistances of the lives of the women who participated in the research which informed this theoretical development, and, which, like Frankl, they have survived and from which they have liberated themselves, will be recounted and heard. It is hoped that their stories will enable those who work with abused women to understand better the depths and ingenuity of the struggle for meaning and survival. These women have allowed their voices to be a means to an end, an end to unhelpful and uncritical professional interventions that may further stigmatise and even endanger abused women.

Before proceeding to hear the narratives of the women and placing them within the wider theoretical developments within sociology, psychology and social work, it is necessary to explore the meaning of domestic violence, its worldwide prevalence and the process involved in leaving such relationships.

Adult intimate violence against women

What's in a name?

Violence against women is an interpersonal experience which has been, over the centuries and across cultures, in turn condoned, tolerated, denied, stigmatised, pathologised, and criminalised. It has also been renamed, from wife battering to domestic violence, spousal abuse to intimate partner violence (IPV), each 'name' representing a reframing of this private experience within the public consciousness. Each title used to describe this private experience carries with it a range of implications, emphasising one or more aspects of the experience. For example, 'woman battering' implies an emphasis on physical 'battering'. 'Spouse abuse' broadens the concept of abuse, but narrows the context of the relationship of the parties concerned to that between legally married partners. 'Domestic violence' is undoubtedly the most commonly used title in recent years (McWilliams and McKiernan

1993) yet this can include abuse between members of a domestic unit other than heterosexual intimate partners. The title 'adult intimate abuse' overcomes this overly broad definition, yet does not limit the context of the abuse to heterosexual partners, and does not indicate the 'directionality' (Forgey and Badger 2006) of such abuse. Hammons (2004, p.280) notes that a term such as 'violence against women' indicates that it is structural inequality between men and women that is the key factor in this form of violence. Radford (2003, p.34) argues that it is important to avoid overly broad definitions as this can result in the minimisation of domestic violence through its reconstruction as an 'equal opportunities crime'. It may therefore be unrealistic to expect one relatively short and readily usable title to capture fully such a complex issue. For the purposes of this book therefore, the titles 'domestic violence', 'intimate partner violence', and 'adult intimate abuse', and 'adult intimate violence against women' will be used interchangeably to name the experience of physical, sexual and emotional abuse, as well as the coercive control of women by their intimate male partners in a heterosexual relationship. The limiting of the focus of this book to violence against heterosexual women does not imply that intimate partner violence only occurs between heterosexual partners, or is always male to female in directionality or symmetry. The debates and complexities surrounding these issues will be reviewed in detail in Chapter 2.

Definition of domestic violence

Just as the title used to name the experiences of intimate partner or domestic abuse has varied over time and across important literature in the field, the definition of what exactly is being referred to has also varied (Mooney 2000). As Wilcox (2006, p.5) points out, one of the clearest definitions of violence against women is that outlined in the 1995 Beijing Declaration and Platform of Action as it is both 'gendered and culturally sensitive'. It also encompasses the full continuum of violence, including violence between intimates as well as stranger and community violence. The most relevant section of the definition for the forms of violence and abuse being discussed in this text reads as follows:

> The term 'violence against women' means any act of gender based violence that results in, or is likely to result in, physical, sexual or psychological harm or suffering to women, including threats of such acts, coercion or arbitrary deprivation of liberty, whether occurring in public or private life. Accordingly, violence against women encompasses but is not limited to the following:

> Physical, sexual and psychological violence occurring in the family, including battering, sexual abuse of female children in the household, dowry-related violence, marital rape, female genital mutilation and other traditional practices harmful to women… (UN 1995, pp.73–74)

More recently, the UN has defined gender-based violence against women as:

> violence that is directed against a woman because she is a woman, or violence that affects women disproportionately. It includes acts that inflict physical, mental or sexual harm or suffering, threats of such acts, coercion and other deprivations of liberty. (UN Secretary General 2006)

The European Union emphasises the human rights and gender equality-based approach to violence against women and points out that the obstacles to exercising women's socioeconomic and political rights increase women's exposure to violence. The EU also notes that such violence is a manifestation of the historically unequal power relations between men and women and adversely affects not only women but society as a whole. Consequently joint action by public authorities, institutions and society in general are necessary for the eradication of violence against women (Allen and Perttu 2010).

The most recent approaches to this problem emphasise the wider dimension of coercive control within IPV (Stark 2007). Stark's detailed history of domestic violence and various understandings of this abuse provide an in-depth analysis of both the forms and purposes of coercive control:

> If the threats posed by equality prompt men to initiate coercive control, its foundation is continued sexual discrimination and particularly women's default consignment to domesticity. To implement coercive control, men must personalise their dominance over women by piecing together the remnants of structural and cultural constraints on which male privilege depended in the past and tailoring the resulting strategy to their individual relationship. (Stark 2007, p.172)

Coker *et al.*'s (2003, p.260) succinct definition captures the overlap of such control with physical and other forms of violence:

> A process whereby one member of an intimate relationship experiences vulnerability, loss of power and control and entrapment as a consequence of the other member's exercise of power through

> the patterned use of physical, sexual, psychological and/or moral force.

Working from these broad and comprehensive definitions, the prevalence of the problem of violence against women will be examined from an international perspective.

International prevalence figures

The World Health Organization multi-country study carried out in 15 sites in 10 countries, found that between 15 per cent and 71 per cent of women experienced physical or sexual violence at the hands of their intimate partners (Garcia-Moreno *et al.* 2006). Up to 70 per cent of female murder victims worldwide are killed by their male partners (Heise and Garcia-Moreno 2002). The United Nations Population Fund report (2000) states that one in three women worldwide have been beaten, coerced into sex or abused in some way, and mostly by a male intimate partner or family member. One in four women has been abused during pregnancy. The European Union estimates that at some point in their lives, one in five European women will experience abuse by a male partner, while 25 per cent of all reported crime involves assaults by a man on his wife or partner (EU 2007). It is the major cause of death and disability for women aged between 16 and 44, accounting for more death and illness than cancer and road traffic accidents (Council of Europe 2002).

In Britain, one in four women will be a victim of domestic violence in their lifetime (Mirrlees-Black 1999). One incidence of domestic violence is reported to the police every minute (Stanko 2000), and it is the crime with the highest repeat victimisation rate in Britain (Kewshaw *et al.* 2000). An average of two women per week are killed by a male partner or former partner, and nearly half of all female murder victims are killed by a partner or ex-partner (Coleman, Hird and Povey 2006). The 2001 British Crime Survey found that 45 per cent of women and 26 per cent of men aged 16–59 reported having experienced domestic violence (abuse, threats or force), sexual victimisation or stalking at least once in their lifetimes, and those who suffer multiple attacks are more likely to be women (Walby and Allen 2004, pp.vi/11). The most recent British Crime Survey (2009/2010) found that 7 per cent of women between 16 and 59 were victims of domestic violence in the previous year while domestic abuse accounted for 14 per cent of all violent incidents as measured by the Survey. Of these incidents, 73 per cent were reported by women, and 27 per cent were reported by men (Home Office 2010).

Studies carried out in Finland, France, Germany, Lithuania and Sweden found lifetime prevalence rates for physical violence, by a current or former partner, ranging from 21 per cent to 33 per cent for women aged between 20 and 59 years. These studies defined psychological abuse as extreme jealousy, restricting the woman from seeing family and friends, humiliating her, economic control and threats to harm the children or commit suicide, and found that such experiences were reported by 11.6 per cent of women in Sweden, 14.3 per cent in Germany, 16.5 per cent in Finland, 24.3 per cent in France and 28.6 per cent in Lithuania (Schröttle *et al.* 2006).

In the United States data from the Behavioural Risk Factor Surveillance 2005 Survey found that 24 per cent of women aged 18 years or older had experienced threatened, attempted, or completed physical violence or unwanted sex by a current or former intimate partner (Centres for Disease Control and Prevention (CDC) 2008). The National Coalition Against Domestic Violence reports that on average ten women die at the hands of intimate partners each day (Wood 2001). In Canada there were 28,000 incidents of spousal violence reported to the police in 2004, of which 84 per cent involved female victims and 16 per cent involved male victims (Ogrodnik 2006).

Irish prevalence studies

To date there have been only two national prevalence studies on domestic violence carried out in Ireland. The first of these, *Making the Links* (Kelleher and Associates 1995) was commissioned by the national voluntary campaigning and service organisation, Women's Aid. The study found that 18 per cent of women who had ever been in an intimate relationship with a man, had experienced abuse of either a physical, sexual or emotional nature. A total of 13 per cent experienced emotional abuse, 10 per cent had experienced actual physical abuse, 9 per cent threats of such abuse, while 4 per cent reported sexual abuse and assault, and 2 per cent had their property damaged.

The second and most recent prevalence study, *Domestic Abuse of Women and Men in Ireland* (Watson and Parsons 2005), was commissioned by the National Crime Council of Ireland and carried out by the Economic and Social Research Institute. In response to recent academic and other commentary regarding the abuse of men within intimate relationships (McKeown and Kidd 2003; Archer 2000) this 2005 study set out to be gender neutral in its sampling and analysis, surveying both men and women on their experiences of abuse within an intimate relationship. A nationally representative sample of 3077 men and women were surveyed by telephone about their lifetime victimisation experiences in relation to intimate partner violence. Respondents were asked if they had been subjected to specific acts of physical, sexual or emotional abuse, how frequently the acts had occurred and the physical and/or psychological impact of these acts. The analysis distinguishes between minor and severe abuse defining the latter as 'a pattern of physical, emotional or sexual behaviour between partners in an intimate relationship that causes, or risks causing, significant consequences for the person affected' (Watson and Parsons 2005, p.23). When looking at the prevalence of either severe or minor incidents of any form of abuse, 29 per cent of the women and 26 per cent of the men had experienced some form of abuse (at some point in their lives).

Using the definition of severe abuse alone, the study found a 15 per cent lifetime prevalence of severe IPA for women and 6 per cent for men: 1 woman in 11 had experienced severe physical abuse; 1 in 12 severe sexual abuse; 1 in 13 severe emotional abuse. This figure of 15 per cent is somewhat lower than the 18 per cent found in *Making the Links* (Kelleher and Associates 1995), and is considerably lower than figures cited above for other Western countries discussed above. It is not possible to say with certainty whether there is a genuinely lower risk of being severely abused in Ireland, or whether the nature of the definition used to delimit this category has resulted in more restricted findings.

The study also identified a number of factors which increased the risk of experiencing domestic abuse (Watson and Parsons 2005, pp.24–25):

- *Being female*: (Women were over twice as likely to experience severe sexual abuse, and seven times more likely to experience sexual abuse.)
- *Being young*: (For women the risk of experiencing abuse declined 15% every 10 years.)
- *Having parents who were abusive to each other*: (For both women and men, this doubled the risk of being abused.)
- *Not being allowed to make decisions about money in the relationship*: (the risk of severe abuse increased sevenfold for women whose partners controlled the decision making about money.)
- *Having children*: (The risk increased threefold for women who had ever had children.)
- *Being isolated from family and neighbourhood support*: (The risks increased by 27% for those living in an urban rather than a rural area, and by 75% for those born outside Ireland.)

Women's responses to intimate partner violence

Liz Kelly has made a number of important contributions to contemporary understandings of intimate partner violence. In a paper presented in 1995, she developed a conceptual framework to help professionals understand the processes women go through when experiencing intimate partner abuse and outlines the manner in which these processes influence her decision to leave or stay in the relationship. She calls this framework 'crisis intervention', but this is not based on the traditional social work intervention method.

In this framework, Kelly recognises that what is done at a time of crisis can either enhance or diminish an individual's coping mechanism, and therefore must be informed by an awareness of coping strategies which they have previously or are currently employing. Kelly emphasises that whatever action is taken (which may or may not involve taking criminal or civil proceedings) it must be premised on the requirement that 'it shifts the dynamics of power and control in the woman's favour' (Kelly 1995). She outlines the variety of strategies which women use to cope with interpersonal violence, both defensive and assertive strategies, and which lead her to reject the simplistic dichotomy between 'victim' and 'survivor'. She suggests that as women negotiate their responses to safety they move through a number of 'processes' (which she stresses are not 'stages', as they do not represent an orderly progression, but are more fluid) from the time the first episode of abuse occurs to the time they negotiate safety. Crisis interventions must therefore be appropriately tailored to the specific needs of the woman depending on which process she is engaged with. She identifies these six processes:

1. *Managing the situation*: This occurs when the violence or abuse is first experienced in the relationship, and while some women leave at this point, the majority do not. Those who stay must develop strategies to manage the situation, which usually involve managing the environment (and her partner) in order to reduce the potential for conflict.

2. *Distortion of perspective*: As the violence continues, her daily routine becomes dominated by the need to continue to manage the situation, and will involve the acceptance of responsibility for the abuse and its consequences.

3. *Defining abuse*: After a number of assaults, the woman may come to define the abuse as violence, which implies naming her partner as an abuser and herself as an 'abused woman'. This involves placing

responsibility for the abuse with her partner, and a recognition that the abuse is not just an 'aberration, but a recurring feature of the relationship'.

4. *Re-evaluating the relationship*: This recognition leads to a re-evaluation of the relationship, and the coping strategies continue in a changed context of meaning. It is now possible to contemplate the process of leaving either temporarily or permanently.
5. *Ending the relationship*: This process may require a number of attempts to leave as the barriers to doing so are complex. (As will be seen in other work, particularly in that of Kirkwood (1993), the process of leaving is influenced by a number of abuse-related, economic and interpersonal factors.)
6. *Ending the violence*: This is a recognition that ending a relationship does not necessarily imply an end to the violence, and may in fact lead to a greater risk of violence for women (Kelly 1995).

While recognising that women move through these processes at differing paces, it is noteworthy that Kelly seems to imply that ending and leaving the relationship follows on from a re-evaluation of the relationship as violent. Such an assumption is challenged by Peled *et al.* (2000) who maintains that leaving and returning a number of times can also be an effective means of maintaining safety and exerting some control over the violent relationship.

Stages of change

An alternative approach to understanding women's responses to domestic abuse has utilised Prochaska *et al.*'s (1994) Stages of Change Model (SOC). This model is also known as the Transtheoretical Model of Change (TM). It is particularly popular in medical and nursing settings. Table 1.1 provides an adapted approach to the Stages of Change Model as it pertains to abused women.

Table 1.1 The Stages of Change Model

Stages of change	Woman's belief	Professionals' 'nudging' strategies
Pre-contemplation	My relationship is not a problem.	Learn about the relationship. Tell me how you and your partner handle conflict in your relationship.
Contemplation or ambivalence	I know the violence is a problem, but I need to stay in the relationship.	Discuss the ambivalence. What are the good things about your relationship? What are the not so good things? How would you change things if you could?
Preparation	The violence is a problem, and I'm planning some changes.	Offer support and encouragement. Clarify plans. List community resources. Provide anticipatory guidance.
Action	I am making changes to end the violence.	Offer support and encouragement. List community resources. Provide anticipatory guidance. Review coping strategies.
Maintenance	I have adapted to the changes.	Offer support. Review need for community resources. Discuss coping strategies.
Reassessment	I cannot maintain this change.	Remain positive and encouraging. Discuss efforts learned from the effort. Review Safety Plan. Remain open for future discussions.

Adapted from 'Stages of Change' (Prochaska et al. 1994)

A number of studies have explored the usefulness of this model to the experiences of women seeking to end abuse in their relationship. In a qualitative study with 19 women, Khaw and Hardesty (2007) also used the SOC model to trace women's decision making and actions in leaving violent relationships. In order to make the SOC model more relevant to the complex process of leaving, they incorporated the concept of 'turning points' which they claim has received 'scant attention' in the domestic violence literature to date. Using both these concepts, they identified three different trajectories of leaving abusive relationships. In recognising the non-linear processes of leaving abusive relationships, Chang *et al.* (2006) concluded that stage-based models may not be appropriate because of the 'non-linear' process of leaving abusive partners. Anderson and Saunders (2003) point out that the model is likely to be of little help to women who may wish to achieve safety and still remain in the relationship.

Leaving as process

Kirkwood (1993) uses the 'leaving as process' approach to women's efforts to seek safety from abuse. Kirkwood's (1993) study, using data from a sample of British and US women, examines in detail the effects of emotional and physical abuse on women's journeys out of an abusive relationship and on the challenges they face in rebuilding their lives as separated/single women. Uniquely in such studies, she emphasises this latter aspect because 'the social context of abuse does not simply affect women who are being abused but also is experienced by women who have acted to free themselves from abuse' (p.33).

Kirkwood (1993) proposes the analogy of a 'web', to analyse both the experience of an abusive relationship and the complex journey that women take in seeking safety and escaping the relationship. She uses the analogy of inward and outward spirals within the web to describe the way in which women's strategies shift the balance of power and control between themselves and their abusers. 'Inward movement' marks an increase in control by her abuser, while 'outward movement' is marked by a decrease in control. She identifies two ways in which this change in direction can occur: first when the woman recognises that her self-esteem and self-worth are being damaged, or that her physical wellbeing is being threatened, and second, when there is a change in her energy level, which she believes can often lead to the woman leaving the relationship. This change can be motivated by anger or fear, which is accompanied by the need for self-preservation or protection for her children.

Inward and outward movement along this spiral is not mutually exclusive, as a woman may be moving outward in one sphere (e.g. economic), and inward on another (e.g. diminished social contact). It is likely, as she points out, that outward movements will elicit responses from the abuser which will serve to pull the woman into an inward spiral again. She emphasises that this model of the web and the bi-directional spiralling movements are not meant to be used as 'assessment tools', or in any way to suggest that there is a normative pattern that all women must follow. She presents the model as a means of depicting the complexity and 'the depth of the process' that women in her study described.

Kirkwood's study is helpful in drawing attention to the effects of emotional abuse on women's efforts to seek safety, and to the fact that these efforts are not represented by one single decisive moment or action. Leaving abusive partners is a process rather than an event, and is influenced both before leaving and for a considerable amount of time after leaving, by the effects of the emotional and physical abuse, as well as by the influences of the social networks, both personal and public, which she reports 'were largely described as judgemental or dismissive. (Kitwood 1993, p.132)' As Anderson and Saunders (2003, p.172) comment, in their review of 28 qualitative studies and 23 quantitative studies which have explored the issues that women face when leaving abusive relationships, the question that requires an explanation is, 'How does she ever manage to leave given all the strikes against her?' This is one of the questions that this book also sets out to explore. The narrative therapy approach to working with abused women which will be outlined in later chapters is an effective counselling approach to exploring women's responses and options as they work their way through these processes, moving backward and forwards through the 'web', searching for support from both informal and formal sources.

The primary motivation for the research which informs the theoretical analysis and practice approaches discussed in later chapters was to seek a better understanding of the responses of abused women to intimate partner abuse and to seek to articulate these responses faithfully within a context which can contribute to improved professional practice interventions. This goal has informed the research methodology and the development of the approach to practice outlined in the later chapters.

Background to the research

This goal of faithfully hearing and representing the voices of abused women was fulfilled by means of the findings of research which analysed the data from 19 in-depth qualitative interviews with ten women whom have experienced and left an abusive relationship. The methodological approach to these interviews was informed by both feminist standpoint theory (which approaches research with women as seen from women's own perspectives), (Harding 1993) and constructivist grounded theory (this approach to research emphasises the meaning of experiences, and builds research from the ground up, rather than proposing hypotheses to be proven) (Charmaz 2005). The feminist analysis (Wood 2001; Kirkwood 1993; Dobash and Dobash 1979) has become one of the most important explanatory theories during the past two decades, and it will be shown in Chapter 2 that any theoretical model on the causality of this violence would be deficient in not including this analysis. In view of the importance therefore of the contribution of both feminist theory and feminist activism in the development of public concern and services for abused women, one must inevitably ask, can feminist theorising assist in the development of an appropriate research methodology when researching this issue?

Maynard (1994, p.14) summarises the feminist research task succinctly: 'Feminism must begin with experience, it has been argued, since it is only from such a vantage point that it is possible to see the extent to which women's worlds are organised in ways which differ from those of men.' In response to this need to see the world from women's vantage points, feminist standpoint theory suggested an alternative approach to research methodology. In contrast to the detached and analytically oriented approach to science and the production of objective knowledge, standpoint research, it was believed, 'would lead to a holistic, integrated, connected knowledge' (Millen 1997, p.72).

Postmodern / poststructural feminist theories

As well as their profound influence on every aspect of contemporary human sciences, postmodern and poststructural theories have also made important contributions to feminist theory. (Postmodern theories suggest that there is no one reality – that reality is seen through the language and culture of the person involved.) Harding understands these latter theories as contributing to a 'voiding' of the possibility of a feminist science, to be replaced by the multiple stories women tell about the knowledge they have (in Olesen 2000, p.223). From the perspective of postmodernism, there cannot be one universal truth. Truth is rather located only in the values and interests of particular groups. Consequently, any attempt to establish a universal truth or theory is oppressive or an illusion (Letherby 2003). Such a postmodernist approach has been criticised as 'relativist' (i.e. changeable), and in its strictest interpretation, makes an impossibility of theory building for practice in any unified sense.

The following criteria have been identified as necessary in research undertaken about and with women from a feminist standpoint approach:

- Feminist research tries to take women's needs, interests and experiences into account and aims at being instrumental in improving women's lives in one way or another (Duelli-Klein 1983, p.90).
- It should provide understandings of women's experiences as they understand it, interpreted in the light of feminist conceptions of gender relations (Ramazanoglu 1989).
- Feminist research methods are methods used in research projects by people who identify themselves as feminist or as part of the women's movement (Reinharz 1992, p.6).
- Feminist research uses both women's own 'different' experience as its point of departure and processes this experience in a manner which leads to liberating knowledge (Lundgren 1995, p.25).
- It values the private and personal as worthy of study (Letherby 2003, p.73).
- It develops non-exploitative relationships within research (Letherby 2003, p.73).
- It values reflexivity and emotion as a source of insight as well as an essential part of research (Letherby 2003, p.73).

Constructivist grounded theory

Qualitative methods are generally viewed as being sensitive to women's experiences as seen from their perspectives, and as empowering in the transformative challenge to research (Henwood and Pidgeon 1992). The methodological approach chosen to fulfil the needs of this research project as outlined above is constructivist grounded theory. Grounded theory methodology moved social science research away from the researching of hypotheses to see if they are true to an 'inductive' approach in which the meanings which individuals constructed for things and relationships in their environment could be formulated in an emergent manner (Whiteley 2004). In this way, theory is generated from data, or may elaborate and modify existing (grounded) theories if they seem appropriate to an area of investigation (Strauss and Corbin 1998).

Charmaz's constructivist grounded theory takes a 'middle ground' between positivism (i.e. the belief that reality is definite and real and postmodernism, as it 'assumes the relativism of multiple social realities, recognises the mutual creation of knowledge by the viewer and the viewed, and aims towards interpretive understanding of subject's meanings' (Charmaz 2003, p.250). The concept of 'theoretical sampling' according to Charmaz (2003, p.265) represents a defining property of grounded theory. The aim of theoretical sampling is to refine ideas, and to test the fit and relevance of the categories and themes. Returning to the participants for a second interview facilitated theoretical sampling by permitting the researcher to explore the tentative theoretical framework which appeared to be emerging from the conceptual analysis. The second interview also facilitated the collaborative methodology which maximised the participant's voice and representation in the research. (For a more detailed description of this methodology, see Appendix, or Allen 2011.)

From these perspectives, the voices of the women who participated in this book provide the original data from which a new approach to understanding the experiences of women, as they strategise their own and their children's safety, was developed. These data and the theory building to which it will contribute, will be contextualised within existing research on such violence and both women's and professionals' responses to it. From both these sources of data, three interdependent concepts – identity, meaning and resistance – will be identified as providing a 'prism' by means of which women's strategies on their journeys from abuse to safety will be recognised and acknowledged. From these three concepts, a narrative counselling approach which can be used by social workers, counsellors and other professionals working with abused women will be presented.

Summary

This introductory chapter has summarised the contemporary definitions of intimate partner violence. It has given an overview of the international prevalence statistics of this form of violence. It has also summarised three of the theoretical approaches to understanding the process of women's decision making in the face of such violence and abuse. The professional interventions proposed later in this book are based entirely on the analysis of the participants' narratives. Hearing these voices with as little professional 'interpretation' as possible was one of the challenges of this research. The methodology used to carry out the research was therefore outlined as it approached the recording of the women's voices from a distinct methodological standpoint. It is to be hoped therefore that their voices will contribute to the development of social work and counselling practice theory and responses in a manner which respects and reflects the voices of abused women and the meanings they themselves construct for their responses to their abusive experiences.

Chapter 2

Complexities Surrounding Intimate Partner Violence

Before beginning to work with abused women it is necessary to understand the current debates and controversies within the field. It is important to be aware and fully informed of these debates, as the complexity of violence against women cannot be fully understood without an understanding of the causality of such abuse. To work with abused women without such an understanding will lead practitioners to approach the issue of intimate partner violence from a perspective that does not fully comprehend the dynamics and consequences of such abuse. It is also necessary to be fully aware of the issue of gender symmetry in such violence, as this is an issue which is attracting a considerable amount of media attention, and without a full research-based understanding of this debate, practitioners may be tempted to adopt the somewhat simplistic approaches one can read in the media.

There are two contentious debates which are of importance to professionals working with victims of abuse. The first is that of the aetiology or causes of such abuse. Is it caused by upbringing – the cycle of violence argument? Is it caused by alcohol use? Is it about unequal access to social power as suggested by the European Union? It is necessary to be familiar with these issues before one can fully understand the dynamics of such abuse and work effectively with abused women. The second more recent debate concerns the 'symmetry' of such violence? There are now many writers who strongly suggest that intimate partner violence is 'gender neutral' or that there is a 'gender symmetry' in such violence. These arguments have been persuasively made and can also impact on resource allocations and professional interventions. It is therefore important that professionals are aware of the arguments and counter-arguments being put forward in this very divisive debate. To not be aware of the research behind these arguments, and the complexities of the issues involved can lead practitioners to believe partners' explanations for their abusive behaviours, which if believed, will make effective therapeutic interventions impossible for abused women. This chapter will explore these two contemporary debates and will outline the principle arguments being proposed in each.

What are the cause(s) of intimate partner violence?

In developing an understanding of intimate partner violence, the most central question for practitioners is that of causality. Are there identifiable sociological or psychological factors which can be reliably identified as contributing to, or even directly facilitating, some men to abuse their female intimate partners? The question of causality is of core importance as the theories one adopts in answer to this question will colour one's practice interventions with women and with abusers and will influence wider social and legal sanctions. Despite the importance of the question however, there is no consensus about the answer in either the research or practice literature. 'A variety of theoretical frameworks have been invoked to explain men's abuse of their partners' (Birns *et al.* 1994, p.50). This 'variety' has not been without controversy.

The debate on the aetiology of male intimate violence against women can be broadly distinguished between two separate approaches. Within these approaches, the work of US family violence researchers Straus and Gelles (1980, 1990) could be described as the ideological mirror image of Dobash and Dobash (1979). The former, and those who work in the sociological tradition, have been described as the 'family violence perspective' as distinct from the latter who are recognised as being in the 'feminist perspective'.

The 'family violence' approach

The family violence perspective can be traced in large part to the work of Gelles (1974) and Straus (1977) in the 1970s when they developed quantitative methodologies to examine a variety of family violence issues. Gelles was the first, in 1974, to point to the high level of violence in American families. Theoretically they take a structuralist sociological approach to elucidate the role of age, sex, race, ethnicity and socioeconomic position in family violence. One of the main arguments within this approach is that stress, particularly socioeconomic stress, is a primary cause of intimate partner violence.

Social stress as an explanation for violence

Within the family violence perspective, social stress is perhaps the explanation most commonly proposed by both professionals and the general public. Theoretical approaches to understanding stress and its effects on families can be traced to the 1930s and the work of Angell (1936) and Cavan and Ranck (1938). Straus (1990, pp.181–201) analysed the results of the 1985 National Family Violence (NFV) survey to assess the extent to which social stress is associated with spousal violence. Using an adaptation of the Holmes and Rahe (1967) scale to measure the social stressors experienced by the respondents during the previous year (e.g. death or illness of a relative, or socioeconomic factors), he found that the higher the stress score, the higher the rate of assault between spouses. While arguing that a major cause of violence in families is a high level of stress, he points out that most of the couples in the sample who were subject to high degrees of stress were not violent. This finding suggests that the relationship between stress and violence may not be causal and he concedes that his conclusions are 'not proved by the findings'. Straus recognises that violence is only one of many possible responses to stress and suggests a number of mediating variables to explain his findings. These variables include exposure to violence in childhood, social support and approval of violence. The most important of these variables was approval of slapping a spouse, with a 456 per cent difference in the rate of assault by husbands who approved of slapping their spouse.

Socioeconomic stress factors

Socioeconomic factors such as low income, low educational achievement and criminality, have also been perceived as variables in family violence statistics, both as causative factors in their own right and as the mediators between stress and violence (Heise and Garcia-Moreno 2002). A range of international studies have shown that women living in poverty are at higher risk of assault than those with higher socioeconomic status. In the United States, both the 1975 and the 1985 NVF surveys found that violence is more common amongst blue-collar than white-collar workers (Straus 1980; Stets and Straus 1990). In Nicaragua, a population-based study by Ellesberg *et al.* (1999) found that wife abuse was significantly associated with being poor and having four or more children. Similar results were found in Cambodia (Nelson and Zimmermann 1996). In India, Martin *et al.* (1999), in a study which interviewed married men, found that poverty (along with other 'stress-related' variables such as low education level and having a large number of children) was positively associated with physical and sexual violence against their wives.

Watson and Parsons' (2005) Irish national prevalence study explored the risk of severe abuse by the respondents' socioeconomic status. Their analysis showed that the lowest lifetime risk for both men and women was found amongst the managerial/professional and clerical groups while the highest risk for women was found amongst routine workers and women working in services or semi-skilled occupations. They point out, however, that these figures cannot be taken at face value, as these differences by socioeconomic group are not statistically significant when other factors such as age, marital status and decision making within the relationship are controlled. Their analysis of the relationship between household income and risk of abuse further emphasises the complexity of the connection between socioeconomic factors and intimate partner violence. While they found that the highest risk for women was in the households with the lowest annual income, those in the highest income bracket had a level of risk almost as high and much higher than for those in the second highest income bracket. This would appear to confirm Heise and Garcia-Moreno's (2002) contention that there are exceptions to the protection that higher income can offer to women, and that intimate partner violence cuts across all socioeconomic groups.

Social learning theory

The second theoretical explanation within the 'family violence' approach is the 'cycle of violence' or the 'intergenerational transmission of violence', as it is more formally known. In the public discourse this explanation is possibly the most commonly accepted 'reason' for male violent behaviour within the home. Based on Bandura's Social Learning Theory (1973) it proposes that the principal explanatory variable in the production of violence is the belief that people imitate or 'model' what they experience and see. Bandura (1973) pointed to the family, culture, subculture and the media as the primary sources in which violence is learned. Steinmetz's work, *Cycle of Violence* (1977), which helped to popularise this approach, concluded that children learn to resolve conflict in a manner similar to their parents in their interactions and methods of discipline.

As with other theoretical explanations, social learning theory has been heavily criticised as inadequate. The work of Kaufman and Ziegler (1987) is often cited to disprove the proposition that the use of violence can be transmitted from one's family of origin. They found that the rate of intergenerational transmission of violence was 30 per cent, which implies that the majority of those who witness or experience violence do not go on to perpetrate violence. A number of other studies, however, suggest that violence in one's family of origin can be a significant risk factor for the use of violence to one's adult intimate partner. Ellesberg *et al.*'s 1999 study in Nicaragua found that a history of violence in the husband's family was one of a number of factors that were significantly associated with his use of violence to his wife. Black *et al.*'s (1999) meta-review concluded that, even though the effects of adverse childhood experiences may be statistically small, they are consistently found as an increased risk marker for adult partner aggression. Watson and Parsons (2005) point out that the majority (70–75%) of those who were aware of abuse between their own parents or their partner's parents, did not experience abuse themselves as adults. This figure reflects almost exactly the figure reported by Kaufman and Ziegler in 1987.

Alcohol use and violence

The association of heavy drinking and wife beating amongst 'lower class men' is a common stereotype that Kantor and Straus (1990) describe as the 'Drunken Bum' theory. Hotaling and Sugerman (1986) in their comprehensive analysis found that alcohol abuse was a significant risk factor in wife abuse, and Black *et al.* (1999), in their meta-analysis, also report that in all the studies which have investigated this relationship, a significant association was found. Fals-Stewart (2003) found in a clinical study that the odds that a husband would be physically violent to his wife on a day that he was drinking were increased 8–11-fold. Leonard and Quigley (1999) found in a community sample that alcohol use by a male partner was more likely to be present in episodes of severe or moderate violence as compared with incidents of verbal violence. The 2000 Scottish Crime Survey found that in 62 per cent of incidents the perpetrator had been dinking alcohol and in 32 per cent of incidents, the perpetrator had taken drugs.

There is, however, a lack of consensus as to the mechanisms by which alcohol functions as a risk factor for abuse. As Leonard (1999) concluded, 'Alcohol is neither a necessary nor a sufficient cause of marital aggression' (p.132). This is evidenced in the Watson and Parsons (2005) study which explored the role and effects of a number of 'potential triggers' to episodes of severe abuse. In response to the question as to whether alcohol was involved in these episodes, and if so, who had been drinking, they found that alcohol was involved 'some of the time' for 44 per cent of respondents, 'all of the time' for 27 per cent and 'never' for 29 per cent. This suggests that the results do not support a strong causal link between alcohol use and the perpetration of intimate partner violence. For those for whom alcohol was a factor, they found that in over 90 per cent of cases it was either the abuser or both partners who were drinking at the time of an assault.

A number of studies have attempted to disentangle this complex relationship between alcohol use and partner violence. Testa, Quigley and Leonard (2003) explored the degree of severity of physical violence when the perpetrator was intoxicated in a small sample of newly-weds. Their principal finding was that violent episodes in which the husband had been drinking were more severe than episodes in which there was no drink involved. They also found (to their apparent surprise) that there were discrepancies between the husbands' and the wives' reports regarding the levels of violence. As they found no relationship between the level of wives' tendency to 'underreport violence, particularly severe violence', and their consumption of alcohol, they believe that a 'more plausible explanation' involves the men's underreporting of violence, 'particularly of severe violence' (p.740).

Kantor and Straus (1990) explored the relationship between alcohol use, socioeconomic status, beliefs about wife beating and actual rates of violence. They found that while there was a clear linear association between heavy drinking and abuse, they point out that 'it is extremely important not to overlook the substantial amount of wife abuse by abstainers and moderate drinkers' (p.211). They also found that in 76 per cent of violent episodes, alcohol was not used immediately prior to the assault. As in other studies they found that men who held traditional views regarding the legitimacy of 'slapping his wife' were more likely to have used violence in the previous 12 months. They make clear that it is the combination of economic status, approval of wife abuse and drinking that increases the likelihood of partner violence. Heise (1998) suggests that alcohol use may contribute to family violence by providing a topic for arguments, while also recognising that feminists have been somewhat wary of acknowledging that alcohol plays any role in the aetiology of abuse as it may be used as an excuse for this behaviour. Evidence suggests, however, that alcohol facilitates the escalation of conflict into violence, perhaps through the disinhibitory pharmacological properties of alcohol on behaviour. As Graham *et al.* (2011) point out, further research is required to analyse the link between alcohol consumption and the severity of violence, in particular the mechanisms by which alcohol contributes to such increased severity.

The feminist analysis

The feminist analysis of intimate partner violence developed in the early 1970s from both feminist theorising about the role of women in society and from the 'battered women's' movements, particularly those in the US and in Britain. Concern about violence against women and the quest to understand its cause(s) can, however, be found in much earlier traditions of feminist thinking. In an article published in the *Contemporary Review* in 1878, British journalist Frances Cobbe describes (in sometimes graphic detail) the serious assaults that women experienced in all social classes of contemporary British society. She goes on to ask why this 'persistent torture of women' is tolerated and concludes that:

> The notion that a man's wife is his PROPERTY, in the sense in which a horse is his property … every brutal minded man, and many a man who in other relations of life is not brutal, entertains more or less vaguely the notion that his wife is his *thing*, and is ready to ask with indignation (as we read again and again in the police reports), of any one who interferes with his treatment of her, 'May I not do what I will with my own?' (Cobbe 1878, p.62)

In these succinct lines, a 19th century journalist and activist identifies what has become the key concept in the modern feminist approach to intimate partner violence, namely the power differential between women and men, which is understood by the latter as proprietorship and control, and experienced by the former as submission.

The roots of these concepts of ownership and control of women are to be found in the cultural mechanisms which give expression to society's beliefs and values – namely the legal and religious structures and discourses which determine the distribution of power at micro-individual and macro-societal levels. 'Feminist analysis has, as its central core, the premise that woman battering is an expression and a mechanism of the institutional oppression of women' (Kirkwood 1993, p.21). Feminist analysis proposes that patriarchy is the social and cultural mechanism which both expresses and reinforces violence against women.

Despite their many differences, both Islamic and Judeo-Christian traditions both agree on the place of women in the eyes of their male God: 'Men are superior to women on account of the qualities with which God hath gifted the one above the other, and on account of the outlay they make from their substance for them' (Koran, Sura IV, verse 38). St Paul was probably the most influential apostolic writer in moulding the early Christian theological understanding of the roles of women and men with exhortations such as, 'The head of the woman is the man … forasmuch as he is the image and the glory of God: but the woman is the glory of the man' (1 Corinthians 11: 3, 7–9). Later recent religious leaders such as Martin Luther (1531) and John Knox (1558) defended this patriarchal tradition. Knox put his views very succinctly when he wrote that 'woman in her greatest perfection was made to serve and obey man' (1558).

The great secular thinkers of the Western philosophical tradition were no less certain of women's place in society and no less intent on keeping them there. Writing about the emerging debate on the education of women, Rousseau (1762) proposed:

> Thus women's entire education should be planned in relation to men. To please men, to be useful to them, to win their love and respect, to raise them as children, care for them as adults, counsel and console them, make their lives sweet and pleasant: these are women's duties in all ages and these are what they should be taught from childhood on.

Patriarchy and violence

Within the feminist perspective of intimate partner violence the sociocultural context shapes, fosters, and encourages the use of violence to maintain inequitable power relationships in all areas of women's lives, but especially in the home. O'Faolain and Martines (1973) provide numerous examples of explicit permission and even exhortations to husbands to use physical violence against their wives. The following is from the *Rules of Marriage* compiled by Friar Cherubino of Siena in the mid-15th century:

> You should beat her I say only when she commits a serious wrong; for example, if she blasphemes against God or a saint, if she mutters the devil's name, if she likes being at the window and lends a ready ear to dishonest young men, or if she has taken to bad habits or bad company, or commits some other wrong that is a mortal sin. Then readily beat her, not in rage but out of charity and concern for her soul, so that the beating will redound to your merit and her good. (Cited in O'Faolain and Martines 1973, p.177)

Common proverbs from around the world provide an insight into the manner in which violence has been seen as a legitimate means of enforcing male privilege and control over women.

- 'As both a good horse and a bad horse heed the spur, so both a good woman and a bad woman need the stick' (from Italy).

- 'A bride received into the home is like a horse that you have just bought; you break her in by continually mounting her and continually beating her' (from China).
- 'Love well, whip well' (Benjamin Franklin).
- 'A spaniel, a woman and a walnut tree, the more they're beaten the better they be' (from England).

(All cited in Grant 1999, p.164)

Patriarchy in practice

Vieraitis and Williams (2002) reviewed 14 studies that examined the relationship between gender equality and various forms of violence against women (including homicide). Gender equality was measured using economic, educational and occupational variables from the 1990 *Census of Population: Social and Economic Characteristics*. The findings of their review provided strong evidence that there was a relationship between women's inequality and rates of female homicide, rape and wife beating. These findings, however, suggest that simple structural reforms of the position of women by reducing levels of inequality in the economic and political spheres, do not of themselves reduce violence against women. The mediating factors of attitudes and marital power dynamics may continue to 'contaminate' the marital relationship with patriarchal values of control and dominance.

Yllo's (1984) study throws light on these points. This study assessed marital equality on the basis of the relative decision-making power of the husband and wife and related this to the use of violence. She found that the rate of wife beating in couples where the husband is dominant is 50 per cent higher than for wife-dominant couples and more than 300 per cent greater than for egalitarian couples. Commenting on the apparently contradictory finding that violence is higher where the wife is dominant than for egalitarian couples, she suggests that, 'Evidently, wife dominance in decision making is met with physical aggression by some husbands... It appears that for many of these husbands, exercise of control in marriage requires resorting to the use of severe violence against their wives.'

In Watson and Parsons' (2005) Irish study, a similar relationship was found between decision making and a risk of violence. In co-habiting relationships the odds of a woman being severely abused are increased seven times where her partner makes decisions about household money, in comparison to couples where such decisions are made jointly. Where the woman makes the decisions about money, the chances of abuse are also increased, but to a lesser extent. These findings suggest that more than 20 years later, Yllo's (1984) analysis is still valid.

Beliefs about marital violence

The feminist perspective on intimate partner violence can also be interrogated by analysing the relationship between holding patriarchal beliefs and attitudes and either using, or supporting the use of, violence against female partners. A number of studies from both Western (e.g. Australia, Britain and the US) and non-Western (e.g. Israel, Palestinian territories, and South Asian immigrants) societies have strongly supported a positive correlation between patriarchal attitudes and intimate partner violence.

Hearn in his 1998 UK study, analysed men's narratives regarding their use of violence to known women, suggesting that they can be characterised as denials, excuses or justifications. He concludes that:

> Men's accounts and explanations of violence take place in the context of men's power and generally reflect, indeed, *reproduce*, [Hearn's emphasis] these power relations. Not only may acts of violence be understood in terms of power and control, but so too may accounts and explanations given by men in interviews, conversations and other forms of talk. Men's accounts of violence are themselves usually within and examples of patriarchal domination and male domination. (Hearn 1998, p.144)

As one of the study participants noted:

> I wasn't violent to anyone. Except her. In all my life. I don't know why. I don't feel motivated towards violence towards anyone else. I think it were a feeling that I owned her. I owned this particular person and she were my property… (Hearn 1998, p.127)

Wood's (2004) qualitative study involving 22 inmates of a medium security prison in the USA, also explored the relationship between beliefs about gender relationships and the use of violence against female intimate partners. Her findings expose the complexity of social norms and the men's ability to hold two apparently contradictory codes of manhood at the same time. She found that all 22 of the participants believed that physically abusing their wives or girlfriends was 'a legitimate response to being disrespected as a man' (Wood 2004, p.562). A second theme which was closely related to the first was that a man is entitled to use violence to control or discipline 'his woman'. One 23-year-old participant described this in a way which is startlingly similar to the proverbs quoted above. 'A woman's kinda like a dog. You got to break 'em. A dog don't do right, you beat it 'til it do what you say. It either leave or be broke. Same with women.' A minority of the participants also expressed remorse and disassociation from 'really abusive men', while at the same time, expressing beliefs about their right to be respected and obeyed. Wood notes that 'all of the men alluded to what may be termed a "patriarchal" view of manhood which holds that men are superior to women, and are "entitled to sex and other attention from their wives and girlfriends"' (Woods 2004, p.563). While holding to these 'US cultural narratives of masculinity' (Woods 2004, p.568), some also justified their violence on their feelings of not being 'real men' (Woods 2004, p.569) and personally embodying this ideal of manhood. Stark (2007) suggests that the core practices of coercive control are governed by gender norms in relationships, confirming women to the traditional roles of homemaker and childminder. He outlines the pervasive and debilitating effects of coercive control on women, and likens it to the effect of kidnapping and torture.

Non-Western cultures

Studies from non-Western societies have found similar patterns in the connection between patriarchal attitudes and partner abuse. In his work with Arab populations in the Palestinian West Bank and in Israel, Haj-Yahia (2003) suggests that 'Men's tendency to justify wife beating, blame wives for violence against them, and to some extent also hold violent husbands responsible for their behaviour are best explained by their non-egalitarian expectations of marriage, traditional attitudes towards women, and patriarchal beliefs about family life' (Haj-Yahia 2003, p.194). In this 2003 study of 500 randomly chosen couples, he found that his results can be attributed to the patriarchal orientation of Arab culture on issues related to family life, marital relations, and gender roles in the family and society at large. He concludes that his findings are highly consistent with the contention that the approval of wife beating and lenient treatment of [domestically] violent men are 'manifestations of patriarchy' (Haj-Yahia 2003, p.203).

Such research findings from across the world provide strong evidence as to the ongoing belief in men's superiority over women and the use of violence to maintain that superiority despite major national and international claims to equality.

Towards synthesis

Ecological framework

Heise (1998) has taken up the challenge of responding to the explanatory gaps left by both the feminist and non-feminist (i.e. psychological and sociological) approaches to intimate partner violence. She notes that 'a single factor explanation is inadequate' (Heise 1998, p.263) and is unable to explain why 'individual men become violent and why women as a class are so often the target' (Haise 1998, p.263). Her response is to propose what she describes as an 'integrated ecological framework' which conceptualises abuse and violence as a multifaceted phenomenon which involves an interplay of personal, situational and sociocultural factors. This framework draws on the empirical findings of various disciplines which have been empirically found to be related to violence against women. She organises these explanatory factors into layers and they are represented as a series of four almost concentric circles (see Figure 2.1).

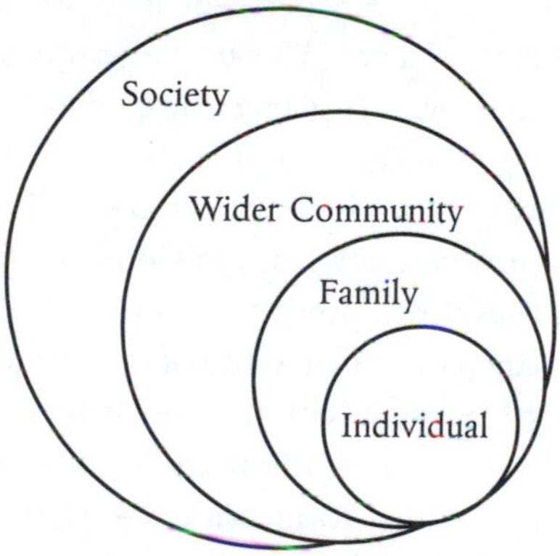

Figure 2.1 Factors related to violence against women at different levels of the social ecology (Adapted from Heise 1998)

At the first, 'individual' level, the man's developmental history includes issues such as whether he witnessed or experienced violence as a child. At the next, family context level, are located factors such as male dominance and control within the home, the use of alcohol and marital conflict. The third level refers to the wider but contingent social structures which impinge upon the individual and family. These include socioeconomic and employment status, level of isolation of the woman and the family, and peer group influences. At the fourth and final level are the widest societal factors such as constructions of masculinity, rigid gender roles, beliefs in ownership of women, and an acceptance of interpersonal conflict and physical punishment.

Heise describes this framework as 'tentative' but as an approach to theoretical synthesis in an area beset by bitter divisions and disciplinary demarcations, her 'ecological framework' holds out a realistic possibility of moving the debate forward and as she says, helping 'activists and researchers grapple with the complexity of real life' (Heise 1998, p.285).

The gender symmetry debate

The second divisive and perhaps more difficult debate within contemporary domestic violence research is the question of whether men are as abused as women by their intimate partners. The debate began with the findings of Straus and Gelles US National Family Violence (NFV) surveys in 1975 and 1985, which found, that while 12.1 per cent of wives were victims of their husband's violence in the year prior to the 1975 survey, 11.6 per cent of husbands were victims of their wive's violence. In the 1985 NFV survey, these figures had changed to 11.3 per cent of wives and 12.1 per cent of husbands being victims of violence. This lit the gender symmetry 'fire' which has been raging ever since. At first glance the evidence of both these studies would suggest that there is an equality of violence between male and female partners, but the difficulty with the findings lies in the instruments used to obtain them. This instrument, known as the Conflict Tactics Scale (CTS), has ignited as much debate as the findings themselves.

The scale is premised on the inevitability of conflict in human relationships and by extension the existence of conflict between all the configurations of family relationships, i.e. parents–children, sibling and spousal. The resulting CTS scale therefore is designed to measure the forms and extent of these 'conflict tactics' within the family, which are divided into three principal modes:

1. *Reasoning*: The use of rational discussion, argument and reasoning.
2. *Verbal aggression*: The use of verbal and non-verbal acts, or threats, which symbolically hurt the other.
3. *Physical aggression*: The use of physical force as a means of resolving the conflict.

(Straus 1990, p.5)

The standardised questions used in the scale explicitly measure the use of one or more of these behaviours in response to a conflict or anger situation during the previous 12 months, but do not refer to the 'substantive issue giving rise to the anger or conflict' (Straus 1990). In view of the sensitive nature of family violence and the perceived difficulty of getting a random population sample to reply to a questionnaire asking them about such private and potentially illegal acts, it is surprising that the 1985 survey achieved an 84 per cent response rate. Straus acknowledges that the presentation of the instrument 'in the context of disagreements' was designed to facilitate and legitimise responses. Presenting intimate partner violence as simply one way in which conflicts get resolved, decontextualised and devoid of any reference to either the motivation or consequences of these actions, has been one of the major criticisms of the CTS.

Critiques of the conflict tactics scale

The primary critique of the CTS has concentrated on what the scale actually measures. Mahoney, Williams and West (2001) query the use of discreet acts of physical violence that have occurred in the previous year and their classification as minor or severe. 'One problem with such an approach is that not all slaps are equal' (Mahoney *et al.* 2001, p.144). Other critics of the CTS have noted that focusing on physical violence alone can hide the atmosphere of terror and fear that permeates abusive relationships. Qualitative studies have shown that many women find emotional and psychological abuse even more intolerable than physical abuse (Heise and Garcia-Moreno 2002; Mahoney *et al.* 2001). Saunders (2002) points out that it ignores both violence which occurs post-separation and sexual violence. Currie (1998, p.101) proposes that the problem with the CTS is that it is 'research rather than theory driven' with the result that even though Gelles and Straus (1988) themselves recognise that power and control are cited by both men and women research participants, these 'disappear from their interpretation of findings from the CTS' (Currie 1998, p.102).

As the debate continues into this millennium, Kimmel (2002) and Saunders (2002) have reviewed a range of studies which have followed on the work of Straus and Gelles, Stets and Steinmetz, and which claim to replicate their findings of sexual symmetry. Kimmel focuses particularly on the meta-analysis by Archer (2000) and review by Fiebert (1997) which cite 100 empirical studies which suggest equivalent rates of violence for both sexes.

Having reviewed the methodology of all of the 76 studies and 16 literature reviews, (including one study which used comic strips from 1950 as evidence of wives' greater aggression), Kimmel (2002, p.1336) concludes that Fiebert's 'scholarly annotated bibliography thus turns out to be far more of an ideological polemic than a serious scholarly undertaking.' Both he and Saunders (2002) compare the data found in US crime victimisation studies with the family violence studies which use the CTS and support the gender symmetry thesis. The former, unlike the CTS-based studies, include sexual assaults, ask about assaults by ex-spouses or ex-partners, and tend to have larger sample sizes (usually national or state-wide). They uniformly find gender asymmetry in rates of domestic violence. One of these large-scale victimisation studies, the 1998 National Violence Against Women Survey, found that men physically assaulted their partners at three times the rate at which women assaulted their partners (Tjaden and Thoennes 2000).

Consequences of and motivations for violence

Hamberger's (2005) detailed review of studies which used clinical samples to compare women's and men's use of violence (e.g. batterers' treatment programmes, A&E attendees, men and women arrested for domestic assault, couples attending marital counselling), found that while 80 per cent of the violence was bi-directional, there were profound differences between women's and men's perpetration of and experience of violence. They found that women were likely to experience greater psychological impact (including much higher rates of depression and PTSD and anxiety), were more likely to be severely injured, and reported much higher levels of fear. Studies which explored motivations for using violence found that women were significantly more likely to use violence to 'protect themselves' (Hamberger 2005, p.138), while men report using violence significantly more than women 'to show the partner who is the boss. (Hamberger 2005, p.139). They summarise the findings of this review of a wide range of clinical studies by suggesting that men tend to use violence 'to dominate and control their partners,' (Hamberger 2005, p.138) while women 'tend to use violence to protect themselves or retaliate against prior violence' (Hamberger 2005, p.139). They point out, however, that there are a small number of women who use violence to dominate and control, and a small number of men who do not initiate violence, do not use it to control their partners, and suffer severe injuries.

Swan and colleagues in a number of papers (Swan *et al.* 2008; Swan and Snow 2002, 2006), have explored the use of violence by women against their intimate partners. In their 2008 paper (Swan *et al.* 2008), they review what they describe as this 'small but growing research area'. Their review of this research leads them to the same conclusions as those drawn by Hamberger (2005). Like Hamberger, they suggest that the research concludes that women's violence usually occurs in the context of violence against them by their intimate partners, is usually motivated by self-defence and fear, and in situations of 'intimate terrorism' they are less likely to be perpetrators and more likely to be victims. They are also more likely to experience negative effects than men. They are rarely sexually abusive, are less likely to use violence for the purposes of coercive control and less likely to stalk their partners (Swan *et al.* 2008). Like Hamberger (2005) they also suggest that interventions for men and women must take these gender differences into account.

These findings are remarkably similar to those of Dobash and Dobash (2004), in their study (which used both qualitative and quantitative methodologies) of 95 couples in which both parties used violence. They also concluded that women did not use violence in the context of control or coercion. Women's violence usually, though not always, occurred in the context of self-defence, and did not lead to as serious injury as men's violence. Men tended to report this violence as 'inconsequential', and they rarely if ever sought protection from the authorities

Why do men disappear in official statistics?

One of the commonest explanations for the clear disparity between the avowed gender symmetry of domestic violence and the invisibility of battered men in police and hospital statistics is by reference to the social stigma of admitting to being abused by one's female partner. As Steinmetz (1977/78, p.503) notes 'the stigma ... which is embarrassing for beaten wives, is doubly so for beaten husbands.' Taft, Hegarty and Flood (2001, p.500), using Australian data, state categorically that there is no 'empirical evidence that men are more likely than women to underreport to police, hospitals or to seek help'. Watson and Parsons' (2005) Irish study found that men were more likely to tell someone about the abuse they were experiencing: 'About half of the women, compared to three-quarters of the men had told someone within a year.' Data such as this clearly challenge the common perception that men are too ashamed to report violence by their partners.

Making distinctions

The last decade has seen a number of theoretical and methodological developments which have been attempting to traverse these competing territories with theories of distinctions. The best known of these developments is that by Michael Johnson (1995, 2006, 2008). His 1995 paper addressed the twin issues of the conflicting evidence regarding prevalence and gender symmetry as presented by the family violence and feminist theorists. Asking 'How on earth could two groups of social scientists come to such different conclusions?' he suggests that they are in fact analysing two different and mostly non-overlapping phenomena. He calls these common couple violence (CCV) and patriarchal terrorism (PT). He specifically explains that he rejects other more commonly used terms and uses this latter term because 'this pattern of violence is rooted in basically patriarchal ideas of male ownership of their female partners... and forces us to attend routinely to the historical and cultural roots of this form of family violence' (Johnson 1995, p.284). Yet in 2000 (writing with Ferraro) and later papers (2005 with Leone, 2006) he has adopted the gender neutral term 'intimate terrorism' for this form of relationship violence.

He identifies the major difference between the family violence and feminist findings as 'gender symmetry/asymmetry, per couple frequency, escalation and reciprocity' (Johnson 1995, p.284) and points to the methodologies used in large-scale representative surveys (such as those of the NFV Survey) as the fault-line in their very different findings. For example, he points out that in the Straus and Gelles second NFV Survey (1990), the average number of assaults reported per woman for one year was six, while in contrast, surveys using the same questionnaire but carried out with women in shelter accommodation found the average per year figure was in the 65–68 range. In order to reconcile such startling discrepancies in data between general population studies and studies of women accessing shelters, hospitals, police and other helping services, he distinguishes between PT (which conforms to the dynamics of power and control, severe violence which tends to escalate over time, causing serious injury requiring treatment, and often separation), and CCV, which involves more minor violence and is less a product of patriarchy and more a product of the conflict issues suggested by Straus and Gelles (1990).

In his 2000 paper with Ferraro Johnson creates further distinctions between differing patterns of violence. Having abandoned PT for IT (intimate terrorism), he adds VR 'violent resistance' and MVC 'mutual violent control' while CCV remains unchanged. He prefers the term VR to 'self-defence', which is perpetrated almost entirely by women, but admits that he 'presented no detailed analysis of its characteristics.' MVC, a substitute for the occasionally used term 'mutual combat', describes situations where two intimate terrorists battle for control, a situation that he concedes is rare and about which we know very little (Johnson and Ferraro 2000).

Support for these distinctions

Graham-Kevan and Archer (2003) replicated and extended Johnson and Ferraro's (2000) study which sought to empirically identify the CCV and IT patterns of violence. Using an English mixed sex population sample, a shelter sample, and a CTS style questionnaire, which, they claim, obtained both self and partner report data for the first time in Britain, they measured physical aggression, controlling behaviour and emotional abuse. Their findings supported Johnson's earlier work and his distinctions regarding patterns of violence. They found that IT was primarily perpetrated by males (87%), while CCV was almost sexually symmetric (45% male and 55% female). As predicted 70 per cent of all IT was experienced by the shelter population. Only 6 per cent of CCV was found in the shelter sample, with 94 per cent of the common couple violence in the community sample. Hypotheses regarding the escalation and severity in IT were also supported, as were the relationship between physical aggression and coercion. The finding that VR was almost exclusively female (90%) also supports the distinctions between male and female aggression in relationships. These findings led Graham-Kevan and Archer (2003) to conclude that patriarchal terrorism and common couple violence differ significantly in levels of physical violence, injuries, fear and controlling behaviours.

Johnson himself published two studies to investigate the validity of his IPV typology (Johnson 2006; Johnson and Leone 2005). In his 2006 study, he has changed the title of the CCV to 'situational couple violence' (SCV). He used a mixed sample (i.e. both an 'agency sample' and a general population sample) to investigate the difference in the levels of violence and control tactics between the four 'types' of violent couples (IT; VR; SCV; MVC) and found that violence was less frequent in men's situational couple violence, and less likely to escalate. There were fewer injuries in SCV than in IT. In men's IT, women rarely respond with violence, while they are much more likely to respond with violence in men's SCV. He concludes that the data 'do not leave much doubt that intimate terrorism and situational couple violence are not the same phenomenon' (Johnson and Ferraro 2000, p.950). In his paper with Leone (2005) they examined the differential effects of male IT violence and SCV. Using data from the US National Violence Against Women Survey which interviewed (by telephone) 8005 men and 8000 women, they concluded that there was a clear difference in the consequences for women from both forms of violence. Women who experience IT are attacked more frequently, the violence is less likely to stop, they are more likely to be injured and to suffer post-traumatic stress syndrome, to use painkillers and to miss work. They are also more likely to leave their partners and to find their own residences or to go to other places of safety when they leave.

Conclusion

This chapter has explored two of the major debates within intimate partner violence research – the aetiology of this violence and the degree to which there is 'symmetry' between the genders in the perpetration of such violence. While sociological, and to a lesser extent psychological theories of causality, have competed with the feminist approach in understanding this violence, Heise's ecological approach attempts to integrate all of these approaches, placing the patriarchal beliefs of societies (and abusive men) as the outer rim of the other individual, family and community factors. Johnson has attempted to provide a similar response to the question of the degree of similarity between men's and women's use of violence in intimate relationships and has developed an analysis which makes clear distinctions between four forms of violence. These findings have important implications for professionals working with abused women and men. They suggest that accurate assessment of the typology of violence is essential before appropriate interventions can be made. Second, they suggest that family background, decision-making patterns by the couple, alcohol use and beliefs about the role of women and men need to be kept in mind when making assessments and supporting abused partners.

Chapter 3

Resistance and Strategic Responses to Abuse

This chapter will explore the emerging literature on the increasing recognition of resistance to oppression and abuse. It will examine the contemporary literature which is bringing this aspect of abused women's responses to the fore, and will use the research participants' narratives to demonstrate how these women used a wide range of resistances as their responses to abuse by their partners.

However, before exploring this aspect of the women's narratives, it will be necessary to introduce both the participants themselves and to give an overview of the abuse they experienced within their relationships. Table 3.1 gives a summary of the women who generously contributed to this work by sharing their stories of the abuse they experienced and their resistant responses to this abuse.

All the women were living separately from their abusive partners at the time of the interviews: Six had been married to their abusive partners, four are now divorced and four are separated (either legally or awaiting legal separation/divorce); four were never married to their abusive partners, and the partner of one of these women was murdered while they were still living together. Nine of the women had at least one child by their partner, one had no children by her partner, but had a child from a previous relationship, and one had one child by her abusive partner and two from a previous relationship. Nine of the women met their abusive partner when they were in their teens or early 20s, and he was the first really serious relationship they had. All of the women were working outside the home when they met their partner (with the exception of Brenda who was still in school), and, as will be seen in later sections, they continued to do so in a number of different ways after they began to live with their partners. While each of the individual narratives of these women is markedly unique, and in many respects the interviewees differ greatly in family background, educational

Table 3.1 Summary of demographic details of research participants

Name*	Length of relationship	Current marital status	Children
Ann	20 years	Divorced from abusive husband.	Five adult children by estranged husband.
Brenda	13 years	Divorced from abusive husband.	Three children with abusive husband, and three by second partner.
Frances	12 years	Separated from abusive partner.	Two school-going children by abusive partner.
Margaret	28 years	Divorced from abusive husband.	Two adult children by abusive husband.
Liz	19 years	Legal separation.	Two children by previous relationship. No children by abusive husband.
Lorraine	14 years	Abusive partner murdered.	Three school-going children by abusive partner.
Phil	17 years	Separated from abusive partner.	Two children by abusive partner.
Rose	10 years	Separated from abusive husband.	Three children by abusive former husband.
Sarah	23 years	Divorced from abusive husband.	Three sons by abusive former husband.
Susan	12 years	Divorced from first husband. Separated from abusive partner, to whom she was never married.	Two children from marriage and two children by abusive partner.

**All names and some details have been changed to protect the participants' confidentiality and safety.*

standards achieved, interactions with family and friends and their use of official and voluntary agencies, the narratives begin to resonate strongly with one another when they recount the patterns of the abuse in their intimate relationships and their responses to it.

Abusive behaviours

The forms of violent abuse and control which the women describe vary considerably, with half of the narratives containing accounts of extreme and life-threatening physical violence, while others recount primarily emotional abuse and control, with fewer episodes of physical violence. However, it is important to note that the form of abuse is itself not an indicator of the impact and meaning it has for the victim. Watson and Parsons (2005, p.72) found that the emotional abuse was 'considered the "worst thing"' by nearly half of those severely abused… even though most had also experienced physical or sexual abuse.' Similarly, Morgan and Bjorkert (2006, p.445) noted that their respondents reported that psychological abuse was more 'debilitating than physical abuse'.

Emotional abuse

Ann met her husband of 20 years when she was 16 years of age and married him when she was 21. During their courtship, Ann found her future husband to be 'very charming, a lovely man'. Immediately after their marriage however, his expectations of her as his wife were established. 'He would expect meals to be on the table' when he came in from work, even though she was also working full time. After the birth of their first child he began to limit her visits to her own family: 'He'd tell me it was my duty to be at home and to look after him and the children.' He was unequivocal in his view of women: They were there to serve.'

Ann's husband became increasingly abusive and controlling. The primary form of abuse, however, was verbal and emotional, and because it was rarely physical, she did not see herself as an abused wife. Isolation and fear of incurring his disapproval became the means by which she was controlled and supervised. 'I wasn't allowed to spend time talking to the neighbours.' When she went to town to shop, 'I'd get myself in a panic if I thought I was going to be late home.' There were also episodes of sexual duress. Control, constant name calling, financial abuse, pushing and shoving and isolation, were occasionally accompanied by more severe physical violence. Ann lays the blame for much of her husband's increasingly abusive behaviour on his gambling habit. When he lost on the horses, 'he'd go around banging things and putting me down.' As a result of his gambling, she did not have enough money to run the household as she was expected to. As in other narratives, her husband controlled what she wore: 'He didn't like me to wear dresses or skirts. He said I was too skinny.'

Ann demonstrated a number of forms of resistance to this abuse. Her careful household management and fear of penury (which resulted from her childhood experiences of an alcoholic spendthrift father), enabled the couple to move out of her mother-in-law's house and buy a home of their own. This resistance coalesced with her sense of herself as a good homemaker with a determination to save. Her main form of resistance, however, was doing everything that was expected of her, 'making sure that nobody could question me… I made sure everything was right.' She also used other strategies: 'I remember one particular time actually, I did stand up to him.' This resulted in 'the silent treatment' for three weeks. On another occasion, 'I went on strike, that was one of my brave moments… He wanted the house shipshape, and I said no… I sat there and read a book or something.' The result of this act of resistance was, 'at two in the morning he was beating me in the bed.' Her resistance involved the strategy of leaving and as with other women, seeking help and advice from external systems, including a priest (who advised her to go home and keep her marriage vows), Women's Aid, and a counsellor.

Margaret like Ann, also experienced 'the silent treatment':

> **Margaret:** That would be from the beginning, he would just stop talking… he'd just go into his mood… and he could go on for days on end and I used to find that impossible. I couldn't take the quietness. I found it very draining, emotionally draining. I remember one time it lasted about three months.

These examples of emotional and verbal abuse, and their impact on the women, reflect numerous other detailed studies. In Kirkwood's (1993) work for example, she explores in some detail the nature of emotional abuse and its relationship to physical abuse. Like the respondents in Watson and Parsons' (2005) study she found that 'in the experience of the women I interviewed, emotional abuse seemed to be a deeper and more central form of abuse' (p.44).

Physical abuse

All of the women in this book experienced one or more forms of physical and sexual abuse, but the experiences varied considerably in terms of severity and impact.

Brenda was still in school, when she met her future husband who was seven years older than her. She describes a positive self-identity and a close relationship with her father: 'I actually did enjoy school, and was doing well in it… and I was very close to my father.' As a result of an unplanned pregnancy and despite 'never feeling 100 per cent great about getting married', she succumbed to her boyfriend's pressure and married him when she was 19. From the beginning they experienced the kind of financial difficulties most young couples with very few resources experienced at that time. Despite her advanced pregnancy, her husband soon became physically violent, following which he would simultaneously apologise and blame her for the abuse: 'And then he'd apologise, but you brought it on. Can you understand what you make me do? And he was saying it was my fault.' The physical abuse, which started at this beginning stage, escalated in frequency and severity throughout their marriage and was accompanied by other forms of abuse.

Despite running a small business together, her husband controlled much of their income and activities. He checked the mileage on the car, and ensured 'everything was in his name'. He also attempted to control what she wore, and some forms of his emotional abuse could be described as 'sleep deprivation'. Arguments 'could last up to 8 to 10 hours. I've often got out of that sitting room in time to get breakfast for the kids.' If she tried to leave the room to go to bed, she was 'thrown around the room… I was getting up every time I was thrown down.' Brenda's husband also physically abused his children: 'My youngest, he got it hard. He was thrown around the place… he started to slap him, and boxed him… and this lad didn't open his mouth. He never once turned on his Dad.'

The turning point in Brenda's patterns of resistant responses was the introduction of a shotgun to the repertoire of abuse. 'I realise, well the guns, I couldn't go back on, that was like the point of no return.' The use of the guns displayed a deliberate attempt by her husband to instil fear in his wife: 'I think it was red and green cartridge he put into the gun. And he had told me in the past he would blow my brains. He told me exactly how he would do it.'

Frances also experienced life-threatening physical violence and death threats:

> He actually used a weapon, that was the golf club. And he had me by the throat… and he forced sex on me that night… he had said that he was going to get a shotgun actually, and shoot me.

These threats were also made during post-separation access visits which Frances arranged so that their children could meet their father:

> And he kept shouting that he was going to shoot me.

Frances believes that the miscarriage of her second pregnancy was as a result of a severe beating:

> Yeah, he knocked me about – boxed me in the back, and kicked me in the legs, and that's when I lost it. I got up the next morning and I was bleeding and when I got to the hospital I was after losing the child at that stage.

While these examples are amongst the most extreme in these narratives, all of the women experienced physical and/or sexual abuse in their relationships:

> **Margaret:** [Whose abusive relationship began with the 'silences'] But I noticed, looking back, six months into the marriage, the pushing started.
>
> **Rose:** there'd be blood and stuff like that. He'd throw me around, throw me over tables, and another time where he continually hit me until I was on the floor. Shoved tablets down me, kicked me in the stomach. And he had me up against the wall, with my feet dangling, by the throat – stuff like that.
>
> **Phil:** Whatever way he pushed me, and he gave me a dig in the back, and I fell and then he gave me a kick – and when (my daughter) came in, I couldn't get up, and he just kept fixing the bike. And I actually began passing blood about two hours later.
>
> **Liz:** The statue of Our Lady, a plastic statue – and he crushed it down into my throat.

While these forms of physical abuse reflect those reported in numerous other studies, what these narratives illustrate is the individual nature of the abusive pattern in each relationship, ranging from severe assaults and threats to kill, to constant verbal and emotional abuse. Recognition of such individual differences, within an overall general pattern, is an essential element in effective assessment and intervention. However, as will be seen, the response to this abuse is also individual and almost idiosyncratic, yet it also reflects recognised patterns of resistance to interpersonal gender abuse.

Control and coercion

Lorraine's narrative places these illustrations of abusive behaviour within a real-life context of control, abuse and fear. Her story contains descriptions of extreme violence by her partner (to whom she was not married) of 14 years. He was a feared local criminal and they met when she was just 16 years of age. Although they were officially together for 14 years, he spent approximately half of that time in prison on various charges, including assault and robbery.

The violence began early in the relationship: 'I'd say it took about six months and I got a clatter then, the first time.' Lorraine was clear that the extremely violent incidents she described did not occur on a regular basis. Many months would pass when there would be no violence at all, yet when it did occur she suffered serious injuries: 'I was sleeping and he wanted me awake. Didn't he burn the tights at my feet, to wake me up.' On another occasion, 'He got the sweeping brush and whacked it over my head… my ma brought me to hospital.' On one occasion, he poured cigarette lighter fuel on Lorraine and on his parents and attempted to set them alight. Such public displays of violence frightened others from reporting him to the police or challenging him in any way: 'And he always threatened me, he'd get them (her siblings) if I ever left.'

Lorraine could not identify any triggers or pattern to his violence. 'He did it with drink and with drugs, but he also did it without anything. So he didn't need either to do it.' As with all the other narratives, Lorraine describes his behaviour as 'controlling'. 'He'd pay the bills, buy the shopping and buy cigarettes, anything I needed, he'd buy.' However, while they always had money, and 'never went short', he would not give her any money to shop for herself. This wish to control his partner was evident from the beginning of the relationship, and was understood by Lorraine as an expression of care and affection.

While he was not in prison they lived on his earnings but when he was, she exercised her agency and worked as a seamstress to provide an income for herself and her children. However, once he was released, control would be resumed and she would immediately 'have to stop work… because there'd be fellows at work.' The contrast between his extensive control of their income when living together and her initiative when on her own is demonstrated by her ability to find work: 'Well, I had two jobs going. I remember one year, I was working in the school, in the sewing factory… but then the minute he'd get out, I'd stop working and he'd manage the money.'

Coercive control

Coercive control can be, and often is, categorised as a form of emotional abuse. For example, Goodman *et al.* (2005) include controlling behaviour within the category of emotional abuse. As noted above it is also recognised as the principal goal of men's violence to their intimate partners. Johnson (1995, 2006) and Stark (2007) identify controlling tactics as one of the principal differentiating characteristics of intimate/patriarchal violence. All of the women described patterns of abusive control, primarily in relation to financial matters, but also in relation to freedom of movement, manner of dressing and self-enhancement, going to, or not going to work, shopping, leisure activities, contact with family, friends and professional systems, contraception and childbearing.

Financial control

All of the women experienced forms of financial abuse, as these extracts from Susan, Brenda, Margaret and Sarah demonstrate:

> **Susan:** He never gave me money. Housekeeping, that was my responsibility, even though I wasn't working.
>
> **Brenda:** Everything was in his name.
>
> **Margaret:** I would come home from work and there would be bank statements, and they would be, for want of a better word – shredded and flushed down the toilet… I never saw anything from the bank, with the joint account… because if you touched [his] money you might as well put a gun to your head… he warned me, if I ever touched it again, he'd kill me. That wasn't my money.
>
> **Sarah:** I don't know how other husbands and wives work out money, but he wouldn't give me money on a weekly basis… I was afraid to ask for money, even for bus fare.

Control of movement and isolation

Frances describes her husband's attempts at total control of her movements:

> **Frances:** It was one day when I was expecting and I wanted to go to my mother's, and he wouldn't let me. And I said I'm going. They're my family and I haven't seen her in about two or three weeks. And he said, 'you're not going.' And I said I am going... that's when he lashed out and hit me. And he said, 'over my dead body will you walk out that door.'

Ann's abusive experiences focused primarily on emotional and controlling forms of abuse, including the control of whom she met and spoke with:

> **Ann:** One time I was standing at the door talking to a girl... and he said Ann, could I have a word for a minute – and I knew – when I came in I got it. 'I'm not going to have you at the door gossiping.'

Liz experienced a similar form of control:

> **Liz:** He just didn't want me to get involved with anybody. In the end, I had to go along with it all. And it ended up that I couldn't talk to anyone... he was always there, present, no matter where you'd go, always with me, 24 hours a day.

These and other forms of control of their partner's movements and contact with others, and a wish to isolate her from family and friends, can be seen throughout all of the summaries of the women's narratives and resonate with much other research into forms and dynamics of abuse (McGee 2000; Watson and Parsons 2005).

Control of personal activities

Controlling behaviour extended into what might be seen as the minutiae of domestic life, demonstrating the exercise of what Dobash and Dobash (1992, p.4) describe as 'the prerogative of husbands'. The control of television viewing within the home was a common focus of this form of control. Susan refers to this form of abuse:

> **Susan:** He didn't like the programmes, so I could be sitting there or the kids could be watching something. He'd come in and change the channel to sport, so we would all have to get up and leave. I was never to forget that it was his house. Even though it was our home... that threat always hung over me.

The narratives also contain a large number of descriptions of control of what the women wore, how they did their hair, and used make up:

> **Liz:** He used to buy me clothes I didn't want to wear. I never wore slacks in my life. I always liked to wear just skirts and that. That was my way. But ever since he said, no, I don't want to see you in skirts. So I had to buy slacks then… and then in the summer I'd always have to wear a jumper, and then the sweat would be pouring off me.

> **Frances:** I wasn't allowed to do up my hair, or earrings… I had to make do with the studs. Nail varnish I wasn't allowed – that was gone – anything 'revealing' you know – like a strappy top, maybe in the summer. No, none of them. I'd have to wear something like a sleeved jumper.

Reflecting other previous work the most consistent form of abuse to emerge from the analysis of this theme was the ubiquitous nature of the controlling behaviour by these women's partners.

Resistance as response to abuse

The use of the concept of 'resistance' to describe women's responses to their victimisation has been evident in the literature for approximately 20 years. The first two important contributions to the discourse of women's resistance appeared in 1988. Gondolf and Fisher's *Battered Women as Survivors* (1988), a study of 6000 women in Texas, challenged the then prevailing theory of learned helplessness, popularised by Lenora Walker's influential *The Battered Woman* (1979) and *The Battered Woman Syndrome* (1984). Gondolf and Fisher (1988, p.3) concluded that 'battered women demonstrate tremendous resilience, persistence, and strengths which press for a less pathological orientation to "victims". We suggest that their experience points to an alternate characterisation – one that considers battered women fundamentally as "survivors".'

Liz Kelly (1988, p.161) defines resisting as 'to oppose actively, to fight, to refuse to co-operate with or to submit', and suggests that it involves women's refusal to be controlled. She distinguishes between coping and resistance, and between victims and survivors, suggesting that the term 'victim' makes invisible the active and positive ways in which women resist, cope and survive. Without this alternative perspective women can be presented as 'inevitably passive victims' (p.163).

Quantifying resistance strategies

In a paper published in 2003, Goodman *et al.* (2003) develop an approach to understanding and documenting women's responses to abuse, utilising a quantitative methodology to enumerate these responses. They propose what they term the 'Intimate Partner Violence Strategies Index' to investigate what factors influence women's use of defensive and resistant strategies and the effectiveness of these strategies in ensuring their safety. The index was developed as part of a longitudinal study of 406 women in the eastern United States, and divided the help-seeking and resistance responses of abused women into six categories: placating; resistance; safety planning; legal; formal; and informal. Allocating each of the responses of the women into one or other of these categories (e.g. fighting back as 'resistance', and getting help from her employer as 'formal'), unsurprisingly they found that women were more likely to use 'private strategies', which they subdivided as either placating or resistance, rather than public strategies such as seeking legal or formal help. They found that women progressed from using private strategies to more public and formal strategies as the violence increased, but did not substitute one for the other. The strategy that was found to be most helpful by 78.9 per cent of the respondents was that of talking to someone in a specialised domestic violence service. Their overall conclusion was that public strategies which involved either family, friends or formal agencies were the most helpful in terms of ending the violence. However, the use of such forms of resistance may serve functions other than simply that of ending the violence. The role of deeper and more complex meanings and motivations need to be recognised as integral aspects of women's responses and resistances to relationship abuse.

In a later paper based on data from the same longitudinal study, Goodman *et al.* (2005) confirmed earlier studies which found that women who were employed or had their own independent homes were less likely to report reabuse. They also found that the use of placating and resistance strategies did not reduce the risk of reabuse. They found that 'women reporting high use of resistance strategies were two to three times more likely to be reabused' (Goodman *et al.* 2005, p.327). Their explanatory hypothesis for this surprising finding is grounded in a feminist analysis of male violence which suggests that when women attempt to challenge and subvert their partner's control, the latter will redouble their efforts to maintain that control through the use of even greater violence.

Discourses of resistance

Researchers such as Wade (1997, 2000, 2007), Coates and Wade (2004), and Todd and Wade (2003), writing from the postmodern perspective, approach the topic of resistance to violence from a less quantitative vantage point. One of the implications of postmodernism's concept of 'deconstruction of discourse' is to bring to greater awareness the use of language in the construction of both victims and perpetrators in the context of violence and abuse. Wade (1997, 2000) and Todd and Wade (2003) draw attention to the implications of language in therapeutic interventions with victims of abuse. In his own work (1997, 2007) and in his co-authored work (Coates and Wade 2004) Wade points out that traditional psychotherapeutic approaches tend to pathologise the abused as passive, depressed or disturbed victims, and, with few exceptions, ignore their consistent use of 'prudent, creative and determined resistance' (Wade 1997, pp.23–26). He rejects both the traditional Western view of resistance as typically based on the 'male-to-male combat' – a view which excludes most forms of resistance, and the traditional psychoanalytic understanding which sees it as failure to comply with professionals' advice. His understanding of resistance is that it includes 'any attempt to imagine or establish a life based on respect and equality' (Wade 1997, p.23). Using accounts of his work with women who had experienced abuse, he illustrates how the choice of questions and the facilitation of in-depth discussion of reactions to this abuse enables clients to recognise their reactions and behaviours as histories of resistance to, and rejection of, the abuse they experienced. Such an approach clearly takes a broader and less rigid definition of resistance than that of Goodman *et al.* (2003) described above.

Language of resistance vs. language of effects

Todd and Wade (2003) develop this approach and provide more detailed explanations of the kinds of therapeutic interventions that inform this practice. Distinguishing between the 'language of effects' and 'the language of resistance', they demonstrate how professional discourses have traditionally concealed and obscured violence and blamed or pathologised victims. Recognising the strategic need to emphasise the effects of violence on women and children as a means of counteracting social myths and conventional treatment models, they suggest that this emphasis 'encodes a number of interpretive biases... which misrepresent victims' responses to violence' (Todd and Wade 2003, p.7). Resistance, on the other hand, is a response that cannot be encoded in the language of effects, but it can be, and usually is, transformed into problems or symptoms or other negative end states. Using further case examples, they demonstrate how depression can be 're-heard' as a form of protest, symbolic of a refusal to be content with abuse, rather than a psychological disorder caused by the abuse. Wade (2007, p.66) cites Bell Hooks (1990) who suggests that it is necessary to locate resistance in the experience of 'despair' of marginalised people. These 'response-based' approaches are modifications of solution-focused, systemic, feminist and narrative-based approaches to therapy (Wade 2007, p.66).

Women's resistant responses to abuse

The narratives provide enormously rich data which elucidate the range of strategies in which the women engaged as responses to their partners' abusive behaviours. The data clearly support Coates and Wade's (2004, p.502) contention that 'resistance to violence is ubiquitous' and also demonstrates the accuracy of Goodman *et al.*'s (2003) comprehensive list of resistant strategies. Before proceeding to discuss how this research builds on and develops the work of Kelly (1988), Wade (1997, 2000, 2007), Campbell *et al.* (1998), and Goodman *et al.* (2003, 2005) the following extracts provide some examples of this 'ubiquitous' resistance by the study participants. Before outlining examples of these strategies, Frances's narrative will be summarised, demonstrating the use of a number of these strategies in the face of extreme and life-threatening violence.

Strategies of resistance

As Frances's story illustrates, all of the women in this book engaged in a number of highly sophisticated strategies to either avoid an outburst or an escalation of the situation, or to minimise the effect of the abusive behaviour on themselves or their children. Because the data contain so many examples of resistant responses, they have been subdivided into a number of subcategories which illustrate the range of strategies involved. They are presented in ascending order of 'confrontational' intent. By confrontational intent is meant the extent to which the behaviour can be seen as a direct challenge to her partner's actions, and usually progresses from avoidance, through verbal disagreement or challenge to outright physical retaliation (Goodman *et al.* 2003; Campbell *et al.* 1998).

'Avoidance'

> **Frances:** I just ignored it, that kind of way. You know, I'd deal with it there and then, and two minutes afterwards, when it was all over, it went to the back of my head.
>
> **Rose:** Now I'd know better than to open my mouth to him.
>
> **Susan:** And I stopped watching my favourite programmes, because he was getting so annoyed.

'Managing him'

> **Rose:** So the more he treated me like that, the better I tried to treat him, so that he would treat me the way I wanted to be treated.
>
> **Frances:** He'd say either do it my way, or don't do it at all. That's when I decided to let him take over the relationship, so to speak, to keep him happy.

These extracts suggest that, far from succumbing to 'learned helplessness' (Walker 1979, 1984) Frances and Rose (and all the other women in the book) are strategically changing their behaviour to avoid abuse, or even more strategically, to change their partners' patterns of behaviour. Campbell *et al.* (1998) describe this strategy of resistance as 'subordinating the self', which they classify as both a proactive, conscious choice and a defensive strategy to avoid further abuse, as described above by Frances and Rose. Taken in isolation, however, Frances's comment could be understood as passivity or even 'helplessness', but as the remainder of her narrative clearly shows, her responses, far from exhibiting helplessness, demonstrate a 'strongwilled' and 'stubborn' woman who engaged in a variety of agentic and resistant responses in an increasingly abusive relationship, resulting finally in legal action, separation and safety.

'Verbal confrontation'

The most frequently cited form of resistance in these narratives can be described as 'verbal confrontation'. This form of response encompasses a variety of verbal tactics to resist and challenge what the women experienced as unreasonable, irrational or threatening behaviour. A small sample of such responses is illustrative of some of these strategies:

> **Margaret:** I was trying to stand to argue my point with him...

> **Phil:** He came in and said something about his dinner, and I said, 'dinner, with what – there's no money.' I'd paid for the ESB and shoes or whatever was needed, and there was no money for dinner left. And he said, 'I'll have me dinner.' I said, 'you go and buy it and cook it.'
>
> **Susan:** And I said, 'you're not working, you haven't got the money. If you'd let me work, we might have a little bit more money and it'd make things a little bit more easy.'

'Strike action'

Downing tools and refusing to co-operate with the demands of their partner was another form of resistance used by the participants:

> **Phil:** ...normal day to day cleaning I'd do, but not a [drinking] session like that – I'd say to him, if you've a session, you clean it up.
>
> **Ann:** I went on strike that particular day. I think something snapped, and he wanted the place shipshape, and I said no, I'm not doing it. Not any more. So they all helped to tidy up – and I thought this was great. When I looked back on it I thought, God, they're actually doing something. And I sat there and I read a book or something.

'Subterfuge'

Subterfuge is a response which straddles the categories of 'resistance and agency'. Once again there are a number of examples of this form of response by the women, in which they take independent action without their partners' knowledge or consent. In the light of the level of control and violence these women experienced, such agentic action is often high-risk behaviour and demonstrates the lack of 'helplessness' in their responses. What is of note in these narratives is that the most complicated subterfuge concerns issues of fertility and the control of reproduction. In view of violent men's attempts to control this aspect of their partners' lives (Campbell *et al.* 1998) resistance to this control is of great significance. The following extract from Frances, not only confirms her ability to engage in elaborate agentic resistance, but these actions confirm her self-identity as 'strongwilled' and 'stubborn'.

> **Frances:** He went mad, he wanted more kids. So for about six months he was going mad over wanting another one... But I said no. I wasn't able for it... And I said to him, I had to go to the

> doctor and see what they could do. And I went in, and I didn't go to the doctor, but I went around the town and came out, and I said, the doctor said if I want to have it (contraceptive device) out, I have to wait three months on the waiting list and then it could be three months after they take it out and then it could take six months before I could become pregnant. And that's what he believed then.

Frances's subterfuge demonstrates the creative use of the well-known shortcomings of the public health system! Phil faced a similar dilemma in resisting her partner's demands for another child, but in her case she actively enlisted the help of her GP in the subterfuge, who, when her partner asked him if there was 'nothing [he] could do to fix her up,' replied, 'I can do no more. That's it. I've sent her to Holles Street [maternity hospital] – it's in God's hands.' Not surprisingly, Phil describes her GP as 'great fun'.

Physical resistance

The use of violence by women in intimate relationships has been the source of a great deal of contemporary debate and has been discussed in greater detail in the previous chapter. Much of this debate has centred on the use of violence as self-defence by abused women (Hamberger 2005; Swan and Snow 2002; Swan *et al.* 2008). This research clearly supports the view that physical violence is one of the many forms of resistance which women call upon in their efforts to keep themselves and their children safe (Campbell *et al.* 1998; Goodman *et al.* 2003). However, it appears to support only partially the work of Kirkwood (1993) and the findings of Goodman *et al.* (2005) that women's violence or violent resistance may contribute to an escalation of men's violence. The latter suggest that 'resistance appears to be a strong risk factor for reabuse even after taking into account severity of violence' (Goodman *et al.* 2005, p.330). In the case of Rose (and to a lesser extent Frances), is it unequivocal that her use of physical confrontation resulted in an escalation of abuse:

> **Rose:** And then the time I retaliated… I don't know what started it… and that started him off. So he took me by the hair and he threw me up against the kitchen units and he was screaming at me.

The following extracts from Margaret demonstrates the dangers of treating the use of violence out of the context of the violent relationship:

> **Margaret:** I gave him a black eye once, and that was purely by accident, it really was. We were fighting and he was – all this shite coming out of his mouth, crap – screaming at me. And I just went like that – across his face – and it was my ring, my engagement ring caught him in his eye, here. And he nearly went ballistic when he saw it. And I just said, now you know what it feels like to have a black eye.

Taken out of context, not just of this individual incident, but of the longstanding coercive and verbally and physically abusive nature of this relationship, this resistant action might appear as 'bi-directional violence' (Forgey and Badger 2006) or 'situation or common couple violence'(Johnson 2008; Johnson and Ferraro 2000) and illustrates the concerns (discussed in Chapter 2) regarding findings from studies using the Conflict Tactics Scale (Dobash and Dobash 2004; Kimmel 2002). Campbell *et al.* (1998) found that half of the women in their study reported hitting their partner when 'fighting back'. Adding to the complexity of abused women's use of violence, it would appear Margaret's physical resistance was not limited to accidental retaliation. In this extract she uses 'strategic' injury, and, as in the former extract, accompanies the physical response with verbal resistance:

> **Margaret:** I actually kicked him in the 'altogether' to get him off me, because he was on top of me on the bed. And he screamed at me, don't you ever do that to me again. He says, look at what you keep making me do! And I said, I never asked you to punch the head off me. I'm not asking you to do any of that, you're doing it.

The narratives show that all of the women (with the exception of Ann who experienced the least physical abuse), engaged in physical resistance to abuse. Lorraine, who experienced extreme physical abuse, contemplated the ultimate form of physical resistance – murdering her partner while he was asleep.

> **Lorraine:** I was sitting on the other bed, like this, with a hammer. And he was asleep like that, so I was thinking of getting him – and I was sitting there and I would stand up, and I'd say, no, what if he'd wake up... and then over in England... I was planning on stabbing him...

This level of resistance, which even though it was not actually carried through, demonstrates the extent of resistant responses which abused women will at least contemplate in their efforts to keep themselves safe from further violence. It also demonstrates her sense of self-preservation in her awareness of the consequences if she did not 'complete' the job.

The strategy of leaving

All of the participants were forced to leave their homes on one or more occasions as a result of their abusive experiences. Some, like Ann and Liz, left a number of times, usually staying with friends, and finally, staying in a Women's Refuge until they secured permanent rehousing on their own. Others, for example Susan, made one final break, also staying in a refuge for a short period of time:

> **Susan:** I'm afraid to be in the house on my own. So, anyway, I went in there [refuge], went home and packed up stuff – terrified that he's going to find me.
>
> **Brenda:** When I was after getting the Protection Order, and they [police] told me to stay out of the house. I wasn't to go back. Their advice was, he's after flipping now he knows you have the Protection Order.

The strategy of leaving an abusive partner has been described by Kirkwood (1993) as the 'outward movement on the web' (p.66) taking the woman away from the centre where her partner exerts total power and control. It can be described as the ultimate form of resistance, but as Campbell *et al.* (1998), Kelly (1995), and the narratives of Brenda and Frances in particular, make clear, it is not synonymous with ensuring safety from violence. The pervasive nature of post-separation violence has been one of the arguments used to identify the particular dynamics of male to female intimate violence (Dobash and Dobash 1992; Kimmel 2002; Pence and Paymar 1993). Peled *et al.* (2000) describe leaving as a strategy which challenges the 'gendered' stereotypes of victimhood, referring particularly to women who return and remain in the relationship. It is impossible to be exact about the proportion of abused women who leave violent relationships, as the assessment of such responses depends entirely on the moment in time when one asks each particular woman about this option. All of the women in this book had already left their abusive partners at the time of the research interviews. The findings of the Watson and Parsons (2005) study support the suggestion that the majority of abused women do eventually end an abusive relationship, but this may be preceded by women leaving and returning more than once (Anderson and Saunders 2003; Campbell *et al.* 1998; Peled *et al.* 2000). As the analysis of this research makes clear, the resistant responses of these women occurred throughout the lifetime of the abusive relationship, and leaving (even temporarily) is but one amongst many resistance strategies. As Anderson and Saunders (2003) suggest, temporary separations give women the autonomy and self-confidence to make a 'final break'.

It is, however, almost the accepted wisdom of professionals who encounter women experiencing abuse, to assume that leaving is the best option for an abused woman (Peled *et al.* 2000) and their interventions are usually focused on her doing so as quickly as possible. Notwithstanding the wisdom of such interventions in times of great danger, the resistance of women to this form of directive intervention is often a source of bewilderment, if not outright annoyance, on the part of those professionals and family members who wish to ensure her safety (Baker 1997). As the strategy of leaving always demands interaction with professional systems (refuges, police, etc.) or family and friends, (McGee 2000; Goodman *et al.* 2005) the women's narratives of the strategies of leaving will be discussed in greater detail in Chapter 5.

Conclusion

This chapter has outlined the various forms of abuse which the participants experienced from their intimate partners. It has also given an overview, from the women's own narratives, of the variety and ingenuity of their resistances to this abuse. This concept of resistance is moving the discourse of women's experience away from that of pure 'victimhood' to that of survivor. However, this alone cannot fully explain women's strategic decision making. The concepts of identity and meaning construction must also be included in these strategies and they will be discussed in the following chapter.

Chapter 4

Identity and Meaning

Human kind cannot bear very much reality.

(T.S. Eliot 1943, p.8)

Woman's identity

Dominelli (2004, pp.76–81) defines identity as 'a constituted phenomenon that is negotiated through social interaction'. She posits this postmodern construction of identity in contrast to the rigid unitary conceptualisations of identity more traditionally referred to in social work literature (e.g. Erikson 1959) and also found in more radical discourses. It is an approach to identity theory which resonates with that proposed by Stets and Burke (2000, p.234) which can address 'agency and reflection, doing and being, behaviours and perceptions'. Somers (1994) suggests that the concept of narrative identity emphasises the embeddedness of identity in overlapping networks of relations that change over time and space, thereby avoiding the categorical rigidity of structural approaches to identity and agency. This view of identity as a fluid progression of an individual's meanings, actions and reactions to both structural and interpersonal interactions, is a particularly useful theoretical prism through which to review the participants' understandings of themselves and their agentic actions.

The concept of identity theory has been strongly influenced by symbolic interactionism, a theory which suggests that human beings live in a world of meaning. Central to this approach is the connection between perception and behaviour, and that the behaviour of an individual is always in pursuit of the goals of the individual (Burke and Stets 2009). According to Stryker (2002), a person has an identity, or what he calls an internalised positional designation for each of the roles that the person holds. Therefore all the women in this book have the role of 'partner' or 'wife', and expect to be treated according to the cultural norms that accompany this role. However, as Burke and Stets (2009) point out, if these norms fail to match the behaviour experienced (as is always the case in domestic violence), great distress is felt and the individual's behaviour is altered to counteract the 'situational meanings' in order to achieve 'identity verification'. Symbolic interactionism also posits that the self is a social construct, and that the self is a result of our social interaction with others.

Burke and Stets (2009) discuss the concept of identity change. Symbolic interactionism (which informs this approach to identity theory) assumes that identity meanings are always changing. Burke and Stets, however, suggest that identities resist change, and that as a result *behaviour* changes to bring situationally relevant meanings into alignment with the identity meaning. These behavioural changes result in a discrepancy between the identity standard (i.e. of being a loved wife or partner) and the self-relevant meanings in this situation. This can result in great distress, as can be clearly seen in all of the women's narratives. If change to the normal expected identity standard is not possible, the only thing that can reduce the discrepancy is for the identity standard to change to match the situational meanings in this particular situation. This is one of the changes to both meaning and identity that women engage in as a form of their resistance to such abuse, which is for them an abandonment of the expected identity standard of their role as wife and partner. They are forced to conform to another identity standard, one which they do not choose for themselves, but which can sometimes lead professionals working with abused women to assume that they are choosing. As Burke and Stets (2009) point out, the stronger the commitment to the identity, and the degree to which this identity is tied to other identities (such as being a mother to the couple's children), it becomes more likely that the identity standard will change and that as small changes accumulate over time, it is possible after a number of years to look back and see how much change has occurred. This can be seen in the narratives of all of the women, as they look back and reflect on the changes to their identities over the course of their relationship.

Liz's story

Liz's narrative can be used as an illustration of the fluidity and reconstruction of identity as a result of social and intimate interactions before, throughout and after her abusive relationship. Liz met her future husband, to whom she was married for 19 years, when she was in her early 20s. Like the other women in this book, she was confident that the relationship would fulfil her hopes – 'Everything was grand at first.' However, Liz's pre-relationship identity is clearly marked by being an orphan, a child who had been brought up in both residential and foster homes: 'I didn't have a family'; and by being a mother herself: 'I had a daughter before I met him.' Her narrative is also marked with a number of references to her sense of herself as 'very good looking'. She had experienced abuse (including rape) during her childhood in care and believed that her marriage would provide her with the happy home life which she never had the opportunity to experience as a child. The emotional and physical abuse began within 'two to three' months of their wedding, and she describes her marriage as 'the most terrible life I ever stepped into'. He forbade her to see her daughter, who was being cared for by foster parents, and then, 'I got to the stage I couldn't talk about her either.' Liz experienced a range of abuse which included constant verbal abuse, intense financial and personal control, and serious assaults. She sought meaning for this behaviour, which denied her the identity of a happily married and loved young mother, in a manner which contrasts her own positive self-image with his controlling behaviour, with comments such as, 'When I put makeup on me I'm better looking! And he used to be jealous of me, saying fellas were looking at me, and all this. And he's hit me and that.' She believed that the fact that she had a child before she was married was also used as justification for his jealousy and his wish to control her. She was not allowed to work outside the home and all contact with outsiders was either monitored or forbidden. She could never attend her doctor on her own, and as she had no family network, she was effectively imprisoned by her isolation and his abuse.

Liz, however, exercised a range of resistant responses to the abuse and control which ranged from verbal arguments, giving up her books, her music tapes and her TV, attempting to reason with him, occasionally hitting him and on six occasions, running away and leaving him. Eventually with the support of a Women's Refuge, she was enabled to separate permanently from her husband. She now lives alone with the support of a specialist housing agency. Liz has participated in counselling to help her overcome both the trauma of her abusive marriage and the traumas of her childhood in care, and says that it 'actually took a lot off my shoulder, because I was carrying a very, very heavy burden'. She now describes herself as 'good looking, and I still am today'. Her narrative is a clear illustration of a journey into, through and beyond an abusive intimate relationship, and the consequent reconstruction of a personal sense of identity in a manner which is congruent with both her self-esteem, her understanding of the relationship, her strengths, her trauma and her recovery.

Perceptions of identity

This journey and its attendant influence on, and reshaping of a woman's identity as she moves into and out of an abusive relationship, can be traced for each of the 10 participants in this book. Table 4.1 summarises these journeys by giving one or two quotations from each woman to illustrate this theme across and within the narratives. These quotations illustrate how the women described themselves when discussing their actions or reflections, before, during and after their relationship with the abusive partner. In this manner they can be utilised to demonstrate how the women perceived themselves as individuals before they entered an abusive relationship, while they were managing and negotiating that relationship, and at some point after they had left it.

Table 4.1 Perceptions of identity at three points in the women's narratives

Name	Pre-relationship	During relationship	Post-relationship
Ann	I swore I would never find myself in that position (in debt), so if I could save, I saved. Left school at 15.	I started working after the children were born. I tried to get ahead of the posse. I was intent on making sure everything was right.	I was never going back to that again. I was offered a full-time job.
Brenda	I enjoyed going to school, I loved sport. I was very close to my father.	I was apologising, for what I don't know. I was still in love with this person.	I grew up through the kids. I keep very busy all the time. I take the bull by the horns.
Frances	Being young and vulnerable. Stubborn. I grew up in a very good family.	I was ashamed, being such a young girl and putting up with that. I used to feel kind of dirty.	I believe in looking after yourself. That's the number one priority, kids, you've got to think of them. I feel I am strong.

Table 4.1 Perceptions of identity at three points in the women's narratives *cont.*

Name	Pre-relationship	During relationship	Post-relationship
Margaret	I wanted to be the perfect wife. I wanted to be drop dead perfect.	They used to tell us we were the perfect couple. I was there (for him) 24/7. Going all the time to keep this man happy. I was terrified. I didn't think I was strong.	I felt I let the kids down because I didn't take him back. I know now that I'm a strong person.
Liz	I didn't have a family. I had nobody. I had two children before I met him.	I just grew out of love with him. I ended up leaving my children.	I was in an awful state when I came here. I was very good looking, and still am today.
Lorraine	I was brought up in a normal house. I was the eldest, I was supposed to be the example. I was working since I was going on 15.	I tried to kill myself. I was addicted.	I was able to tell her what had happened to me, I hope it made a difference. I always talk to people. I do miss him.
Phil	(If you go) with lots of men, you're used baggage.	I wasn't the quiet type. I always could manage.	I think sometimes I should have had a brain transplant. I think sometimes I was an awful eejit.

Rose	I was brought up in a very loving home. A very competent person.	As stupid as he says you are. I was continually looking for his approval. I wanted to be the one to look after him.	I am confident now. I have an awful lot of self-respect for myself now.
Sarah	I came from a sad family background. I had to cope on my own… too much responsibility too soon. I always felt I wanted someone to love me.	I took the responsibility. I had quite a good job. Two children so close, at my age and with my health… I was in a very bad way.	When I left I couldn't cope on my own. I've behaved in a very dignified way. I have been able to stand up to him and come out the other side.
Susan	I was separated when I met him. I didn't have great self-esteem because I'd been through a divorce. I enjoyed working. I was the 'joker'.	I was trying my best to stand up to him. I was trying to keep myself and the kids safe.	I felt really guilty (about the children). I know I'm much stronger now. I will never ever trust a man again.

What is most notable about the women's narratives regarding their identity and sense of self is the manner in which they spontaneously describe themselves, usually in the middle of a comment or reply in relation to the primary theme of the interviews (i.e. narratives of abuse and resistance). For example, Frances used a number of different ways to identify herself as strongwilled. 'She knew that I was too strongminded anyway': and elsewhere, 'I was too stubborn.' In contrast she employs an almost oppositional self-identity to justify her involvement with and acceptance of an abusive pattern of behaviour from her partner: 'Being young and vulnerable' and, 'I was so young I didn't know anything.' She also identified her family background as non-abusive and therefore as a contrast to her intimate relationship: 'My parents never ever controlled my life.' This presentation of a changeable and fluid identity, an identity which is responsive to external and traumatic events, is clearly visible in the manner in which the quotations are presented above. It is as if the sense of self is experienced on a timeline, like stills from a movie in which the characters are redrawn as the movie progresses.

For example, Rose identifies her family background 'as a very loving home,' and like Frances she contrasts this with the gradual disintegration of her self-identity from 'a very confident person' to someone whom she describes as being as 'stupid as he says you are.' She also contrasts her self-identity as 'always very much into my sense of dress' to someone who 'let myself go when I was with him, because it seemed to me that the more dressed up I was, the worse it was.'

What is most significant about the self-identity by means of which the women described themselves is the relationship between this self-identity and the patterns of agentic and resistant actions which they employed as responses to the abusive situations in which they found themselves. Susan, for example, presented herself as a stubborn, independent woman, competent and willing to work. She attributed her partner's abusive behaviour to his heavy drinking, but engaged in a range of resistant strategies in response to his abuse:

> **Susan:** So I said to him, I wash my hands of you. If you come out and go on the drink again, I'm not helping you again… I'm not washing your clothes and ironing them. I made a separate claim (for Social Welfare) because I knew from previous that if he got something, he wasn't going to give it to me.

Ann identified herself as a very careful manager, who took great pride in having her house in perfect order, managing the small allowance he gave her from his salary. Her resistance to her husband's controlling behaviour included saving up enough money without his knowledge so that they could put a deposit on a house, and moving away from the confining environment of her husband's family home. Sarah's narrative contains a number of references to her identity in terms of physical and mental ill health and not surprisingly, her pattern of resistant strategies included devising ways to ensure that she was able to access appropriate medical care for both herself and her children: 'I had saved up a few bob so I rang a consultant in R, and I arranged an appointment. I told the boys not to say anything when we got home.'

These data reflect Giddens' (1991, p.5) description of self-identity as 'a reflexively organised endeavour' which requires the sustaining of coherent, yet continuously revised biographical narratives. He insists that self-identity is not a passive entity, but is continually and reflexively constructed by local (even global) events. Amongst these 'events', are the social discourses which inform and shape young women's understandings of themselves and their relationships. Of particular importance amongst these discourses are the gender and romance narratives such as those which Kulkarni (2007) and Wood (2001) describe. Amongst these dominant gender narratives, Wood (2001) identifies the narrative that stipulates that it is appropriate for men to be controlling and dominating and for women to be subordinate and to defer to men. Somers (1994, p.618) describes such discourses as the 'public narratives' which are attached to cultural and institutional formations beyond the individual. What she describes as the 'ontological narratives' (personal narratives) define what we are and what we do, and are constitutive of ambiguous and ephemeral narrative identities. 'They affect activities, consciousness, and beliefs, and are in turn affected by them' (p.620). From this perspective, social life is constructed through both ontological and public narratives. A fuller understanding of the influence of these narratives on the construction of a woman's identity cannot, however, be fully analysed in isolation from the theme of meaning reconstruction/reflection which will be further explored in the next section of this chapter. What is clear from the data presented above, however, is that the experience of a violent intimate relationship shapes the reconstruction and redefinition of the woman's identity.

Meaning and reflections

As T.S. Eliot suggests, human beings cannot bear too much pain and disappointment. The process of coping with reality, particularly unwelcome and incongruous reality as described and experienced by the participants in this book, is understood as the construction and reconstruction of meaning. This section will explore the women's approaches to understanding the 'meaning' of their relationship as it moved from its happy beginnings through the abuse and violence they experienced, to their decisions to leave and the options they explored in this leaving process. During the interviews each woman was given the opportunity to reflect on their own understanding of their partner's abusive behaviour towards them and how they understood the way in which their partners explained or justified their behaviour. The women's reflective contributions and recollections – what might be called the 'mulling over' of their experiences, or their 'reflexive narratives' (Angus, Levitt and Hardtke 1999, p.1258) – are rich in the narrative of meaning construction and are also related to the construction and reconstruction of identity discussed above.

Rose's narrative of an extremely abusive relationship provides a clear account of the manner in which the overlapping processes of identity, violence and meaning facilitated survival and recovery.

Rose's story

Rose met and fell in love with her partner when she was 21. Her parents did not like him and advised her not to go out with him. When he caused damage to their gates while in a drunken rage, they gave her an ultimatum; she was forced to choose between them and him. 'And of course, at 21, besotted by this man, I moved out.' Physical violence started within eight months. From the very beginning, her narrative identifies the themes which recur again and again – her subject position of wanting to care for and 'save' him: 'I wanted to be the one person who wouldn't walk out on him'; and her shame and embarrassment at what was happening: 'It was too humiliating' [to talk to anyone]. This was made more difficult by the fact that she lived in a small tight-knit community where she knew the Garda sergeant and local GP. Rose felt extreme pity for her partner as she believed he had had a difficult upbringing, and he relied on this pity to keep her tied into the relationship. She saw herself as his carer and in this role she felt she could not abandon him. Rose's narrative describes a series of extreme physical assaults and abuse, as well as constant verbal abuse. There are few descriptions of financial abuse and she appears to have been the financial manager of the family.

Unlike other women's accounts, she makes little reference to positive aspects of their relationship. As she describes it, it was almost consistently abusive, threatening and exhausting for her. Her partner displayed a willingness to vent his rage and anger at her whenever he felt like it, and blamed her for causing him to be so violent.

Her resistance and agency is consistent throughout the narrative, holding down numerous jobs (at one time three jobs at the same time), and insisting that they have a nice home. Her commitment to making the relationship work, while avoiding naming her experience as abusive, is demonstrated by her use of a variety of services 'to get him well', for example, a marriage counsellor, a GP and a homoeopath. From Rose's narrative it is not possible to be sure whether a more proactive approach by any of these professionals would have assisted her to disclose her situation earlier, as keeping it 'secret' was an element of her agentic strategy – as she put it: 'That was a secret I could not break.'

Rose describes a variety of forms of resistance to the abuse, including a loss of memory for a lengthy period of time, leaving him on a number of occasions, getting him to leave, experiencing depression, contemplating suicide, accepting treatment for her depression (including inpatient treatment), and later rejecting it as she recognised the cause of her depression, arguing with him, running away from him, keeping quiet, abandoning her own opinions, and on one occasion, physically retaliating by scraping his face.

The turning point in Rose's resistant strategies was the prolonged and serious illness of her youngest son. This led her to tell her parents the extent of the abuse she was experiencing and she made contact with a Women's Refuge service. This resulted in her taking a barring order against her husband, which he breached and for which she had him arrested. Her participation in a support group for abused women facilitated her reflection on her experiences, reflections which are evidenced throughout her narrative.

Finding meaning

Rose's narrative provides a number of examples of the interrelationship of identity construction and meaning in the context of a partner's problematic behaviour. On one occasion her partner was arrested for public disorder and verbally abusing a policeman:

> **Rose:** I followed them down, I demanded to see him. I said I'm not leaving here until you allow me into the cells to make sure he's okay. I was still very much concerned for him, so [next day] I rang the Garda Station and asked where he was. And they said he's still here… and I said if you don't allow him out of that cell now, I'm going to leave this apartment now, and if anything happens to me between the time I leave here and get to the Garda Station, I'll hold you personally responsible, because you told me he'd be home.

In this extract, Rose's self-identity as his carer – 'I felt I was the one to look after him' – is consistent with her resistant responses to the external (police) system who, in her construction of this situation, were interfering with her role and acting in a threatening manner to the man she cared for and about.

In the following extract, Rose provides an example of meaning construction and resistance in the context of her identity and her understanding of the situation in hindsight – 'looking back':

> **Rose:** At that stage I suppose, looking back, I didn't really see it as a huge problem. *My biggest problem then was getting [him] well. Because I saw him as an unwell man. So we went to a counsellor…* I had myself under a spell with him. I was just totally in awe of this man, and he was very handsome. At the time he seemed very intelligent, a

> great worker. *I wanted to be the last person, the one person who wouldn't walk out on him.*

Rose is here describing the interrelationship between her identity as his carer and saviour: 'the one person who wouldn't walk out on him,' as he was an 'unwell man' and her resistant responses to his behaviour: 'So we went to a counsellor.' Her narrative contains a number of similar responses, in which she interprets her behaviour (e.g. 'to get him well') in such a way that it is congruent with her self-identity as his carer, 'getting [him] well.' Anderson and Saunders (2003, p.175) point out that far from being a sign of passive resignation and acceptance of abuse, responses such as these described by Rose, require active effort 'to construct a particular meaning to her circumstances that will allow both the continuation of the love that she feels toward her partner and endurance of the pain of abuse.' Ferraro and Johnson (1983, p.328) describe such strategies as appeals to 'the salvation ethic'.

Tracing Rose's relationship and the escalation of the physical and emotional abuse, the tension between Rose's self-identity and the narrative of abuse, presents a challenge to her sense of narrative coherence. She captures this tension when describing the conflict between her identity as the daughter from a 'loving home', whose parents 'weren't used to anything of this sort', and who was 'a very confident person' when she met her partner, and her reconstructed identity as a severely abused woman. The effects of this apparently irreconcilable conflict of identities were initially allayed by her reluctance to tell anybody about the abuse: 'It was too humiliating [to tell anybody].' This agentic action of keeping the abuse a secret was also congruent with her narrative of admiration and affection for him:

> **Rose:** ...definitely not [tell] anybody I knew, because I didn't want anybody to think badly of [him]. I know! I know! It doesn't make any sense at all. But I didn't want people thinking badly of him.

By highlighting her awareness of the apparent 'non' sensical nature of her (re)actions, Rose is here drawing attention to her 'rewriting' of her self-narrative, locating herself contemporarily in a different identity from that within her narrative of that time, which was itself a reconstruction of her former self-identity as the 'confident, besotted young woman'.

'The most terrible life I have stepped into'

Liz's narrative can also be seen to flow through the process of both meaning and identity construction and reconstruction. Given her pre-relationship identity as an abandoned and abused child in care –'My parents didn't want me' – she sought an intimate relationship as an escape from that identity to a 'being cared for' alternative which she describes as being 'all I had at the time.' Her hopes were not realised, as her narrative of abuse illustrates, and her response to this was to redefine the relationship itself and consequently her self-identity within it. This redefinition was hastened by the projection of blame by her partner (as in all the narratives). The narrative can then be read as her journey from one troublesome identity to the hope of a better socially constructed identity as a loved wife and partner – an identity which was quickly challenged by the reality of her partner's abuse.

Liz, however, did not adopt the identity of the abused submissive woman which her partner chose for her, but his abuse did force her to temporarily adopt an identity as someone who 'stepped into the most terrible life' – a construction of the relationship which distances her from agency and responsibility for the nature of the relationship. Her response to this enforced new identity as an abused woman rather than a happily married and cared for woman, involved the meaning reconstruction which enabled her to emotionally tolerate and cognitively make sense of the violence: 'It was all over jealousy. I knew he must be jealous of my good looks.' In this sense, her meaning reconstruction can be seen not alone as a coping mechanism, but as a form of resistance in itself.

A similar analysis can be carried out for each woman's narrative – an analysis which would trace the journey from pre-relationship self-identity, constructed in conjunction with the meaning of both her experience and her hopes, through meaning reconstructions, necessitated by the dissonance between her preferred identity and that imposed by her abuse experience.

As Neimeyer (2000a) has pointed out, a constructivist meta-theoretical (i.e. overarching) standpoint would suggest that in struggling to make sense of their life stories, human beings compose meaningful accounts of the important events of their lives, constantly editing, revising and rewriting these accounts when the presuppositions on which these accounts are based are called into question by unexpected and incongruent events. The experiences of abuse by their intimate partners are clearly 'unexpected and incongruent' events in these women's lives, and their narratives make explicit their efforts to 'rewrite' and 'reauthor' these experiences in ways which enable them to assimilate the experiences into meaningful accounts of their relationships.

In the case of bereavement, the process of reconstruction of identity and meaning is ironically facilitated by the certainty of the loss (in death) of one of the significant others by which personal identity is affirmed (Neimeyer 2000a), whereas for abused women, the uncertainty of the relationship and the unpredictable reactions to their self-identity, create great complexity for their construction of meaning. The manner in which the women's self-identity changed from that at the pre-relationship stage, through the impact of the abusive experiences, to their self-understanding from the standpoint of their current violence-free lives, was demonstrated in Table 4.1. This journey into, through and away from a violent relationship demands a reconstruction of identity which is compatible with the impact of the abuse and the resistance with which the women responded to the abuse. In order to maintain congruity between experience and identity, this process of reconstruction of identity is facilitated and enabled by the reconstruction of the meaning of the experience. As Wood (2001, p.241) points out however, our culture provides 'vocabularies of understanding, motive, and significance' to assist us to construct such meanings for our personal experiences. Liz's reference to her partner's jealousy, and Susan's locating the cause of her partner's abuse in his drinking, are examples of their use of such culturally acceptable narratives to enable them to reduce the dissonance between their hopes and their experiences.

Partners' construction of meaning

It is not just the women who construct meaning to explain their behaviour and their responses to the abuse they experienced. The women also describe how they understood the manner in which their partners justified their abuse, as they demonstrate meaning construction of abusive behaviour by men whom they loved and chose to live with. It is necessary to emphasise that these meaning constructions are ascribed to the men, by the women, 'after the fact'. Table 4.2 summarises these data by providing examples from each woman.

These data illustrate the efforts by the abused women to construct a meaning for behaviour by their partners which they found unacceptable and frightening. It was clearly at odds with their construction of what a happy loving relationship should be and was therefore not congruent with their own (or contemporary Western society's) construction of an intimate relationship. The data support much other work which has looked at men's construction of the meaning of their abusive behaviours (e.g. Cavanagh *et al.* 2001; Pence and Paymar 1993). Abusive partners consistently project the blame for their abuse onto the woman, presenting a view of a domestic relationship which is essentially hierarchically organised on a gendered basis.

Table 4.2 Abusive partner's meaning of abuse (as reported by woman)

Woman's name	Partner's meaning (as reported by her)
Ann	…he'd tell me it was my duty to be at home and to look after him and (daughter). Pressing me against the pillows and telling me I was crazy and I'd made my vows, that it was my duty.
Brenda	No man was telling him what he could do. He thought he could do whatever I [he] want[s]. He was saying it was all my fault.
Frances	She's mine, she's the mother of my children, like I was his property. If anyone else will have you, I'll take you to your grave. It was his attitude, that men are the boss. And they can do whatever they want. He believed it was all me. Something wrong with me.
Margaret	Men don't do shopping, those were his words – men don't clean the house. Wouldn't take the kids out or anything… That's for a woman, what else would you be doing? That's what you should be doing.
Liz	He didn't want anyone to have me. He didn't want me to have friends. He used to say all women were hoors.
Lorraine	That's control, I suppose, controlling me. Like you're mine, you're not to talk to this person, you're not to do that.
Phil	He said I had no opinion in his decisions, in what went on in the house, that he was the master of his house.

Table 4.2 Abusive partner's meaning of abuse (as reported by woman) *cont.*	
Woman's name	**Partner's meaning (as reported by her)**
Rose	He'd say it's all in your head, what are you talking about. He had me in any way he chose fit... he felt that he had 100 per cent control over me and he felt justified. He had taken an overdose, and he had blamed it on me, after he got out of hospital.
Sarah	He was controlling me in every way, from the food we ate to the things we bought for the home. If I did something he didn't approve of, I'd be a nervous wreck.
Susan	He'd say no, I was the one with the problem. Everything that went wrong in the relationship was my fault. He didn't like the fact that I was spending time with the kids, or not spending it with him. I was never let forget that it was his house. He said he wasn't a childminder, I'm not staying at home to mind the baby... No, you're not working.

These beliefs expose the contradictory 'public narratives' pertaining to intimate relationships and marriage in particular. While the influence of the public 'romance narratives' (Wood 2001) can be seen in the women's construction of the meaning of the relationship for them, the men's construction of meaning for their behaviour reflects the public narrative of dominance and the assumption that they have the 'right to master others'. 'Most batterers are informed by cultural messages justifying dominance' (Pence and Paymar 1993, p.4). The data can be seen therefore to add to the body of evidence in support of the feminist analysis of such violence. It resonates with the work of Hanmer (2000, p.10) who reported similar findings in research with a multicultural sample of abused women: 'Women's accounts demonstrate that men from varied cultural and ethnic groups have in common cultural and family advantages that come from being male.' Each of the women in this book reported comments or justifications by their partners which strongly support the concept of male power and privilege and a strict gender division of labour and responsibility.

These data also show, as previous work has shown, that abusive men minimise and deny responsibility for abuse as reported by both their women partners (Stark 2007) and by abusive men themselves (Cavanagh *et al.* 2001). Susan's comment that 'He'd say no, I was the one with the problem. Everything that went wrong in the relationship was my fault,' illustrates this form of minimisation and projection of blame. However, as an abusive strategy, this denial and blaming behaviour adds to the task of meaning reconstruction, which, as has been shown earlier in this section, is emerging as a form of resistant response by the men's partners. In this task the woman is confronted not only with behaviour which is incongruent with her meaning of an intimate relationship, but she is also forced to construct a meaning for this behaviour which further challenges and undermines her extant identity as a competent and caring partner in the relationship. In reconstructing the meaning of her relationship, she must now 'counter' his constructions of meaning as well as his behaviours. Such efforts have led the women to say such things as, 'I feel like a leper,' 'Totally exhausted,' 'Like I was locked in a prison for ten years.'

Conclusion

This continual construction and reconstruction of meaning and identity as strategies of both resistance and a struggle for coherence, appeared to have two inevitable outcomes: first, as suggested in the last three quotes above (and as pointed out by Burke and Stets 2009), the women became exhausted and experienced forms of self-loathing. Second, as Campbell *et al.* (1998) pointed out, they re-evaluated their relationship and their futures. The manner in which this re-evaluation led to the end of their relationship has been identified as 'turning points' in the process of dealing with the violence (Khaw and Hardesty 2007). The following chapter will explore these turning points, illustrating them with the women's own experiences.

Chapter 5

Leaving the Abusive Relationship

Turning points

As outlined earlier, all of the women had left their partners at the time they were interviewed. At the risk of imposing undue theoretical coherence on what were dangerous and chaotic experiences, it is possible to identify a 'turning point' in each woman's narrative. As will be seen in this chapter, for each woman there was a 'trigger' event which precipitated the permanent rupture of the relationship. Lorraine is the exception to this pattern, as her relationship ended with the murder of her partner. These trigger events have been mentioned in the summaries of the women's narratives given throughout this book. The following summary of Susan's story includes the turning point which led her to seek a permanent end to her abusive relationship.

Susan's story

Susan was divorced from her first husband before setting up a new home with her violent partner in a rural part of Ireland. She had two children by her first husband in Dublin, and had two children by her second partner. Her partner was also previously married and had three children from that marriage.

Once her first child was born, her partner refused to mind him to enable her to look for work – as he said, 'he wasn't a childminder.' He eventually got work which kept him away from home for one week out of every two, and a pattern of regular heavy drinking and unequal responsibility for childcare and homemaking became established. 'He never gave me money… that was my responsibility, even though I wasn't working.' Her narrative is dominated with accounts of her partner's heavy drinking, which she blames for his abusive behaviour – 'I thought it was all to do with drink.' She describes episodes of volatile arguments, fuelled by his drinking, and in his eyes, by her premenstrual tension.

Financial stress, financial abuse, control and verbal abuse predominate in her account of his behaviour during their ten-year relationship. Her account of these arguments suggest that she maintained a consistent pattern of resistance, constantly defending herself, reasoning with him, or keeping quiet so as to avoid escalating the arguments, 'I would bite my lip.' His behaviour was consistently controlling – wanting her company at all times when he wasn't working or drinking, changing television channels when he came into the house, demanding that she accompany him to the pub even when she didn't want to go. Her resistance included a number of separations, sometimes initiated by him, when he 'threw her out of the house' and sometimes by her. She returned on the final occasion, when her youngest child started 'to ask for his dad,' hoping that 'maybe this separation, being apart, has made him realise and given him time to think… maybe it would work this time.'

As his drinking continued, his mental and physical health deteriorated. He suffered a minor stroke and she agreed to look after him if he stopped drinking. When he continued to drink, their relationship developed into an 'in-house separation'. He lived upstairs, but again, exercising resistance and agency, she declined to nurse him as he wished – 'I'm not washing your clothes and ironing them, you're on your own.' The turning point for Susan came during this period of alcohol-related depression. When he refused to give her the dependant relative component of his sickness benefit, while she was unemployed and had no money to buy food for her children, she went through his pockets to look for some money. This precipitated his one and only physical assault: 'He jumped out of bed and got me by the scruff of the neck and threw me against the wall.' This was a clear escalation in the forms of abuse she had previously experienced. Her response was to leave the house and move to a Women's Refuge, an experience which enabled her to begin the next stage of her life, living in rented accommodation with her four children and participating in self-development programmes.

Pattern of turning points

As Kelly (1995) and others have pointed out, however, the end of the relationship is not always synonymous with the end of the violence. This was the case for Frances, Brenda, and Rose, and as has been shown in their summaries, they experienced severely frightening post-separation abuse and threats. For Frances, Rose, Sarah, Brenda and Ann, the turning point involved implicit or explicit threats to their children's welfare, or the involvement of the children themselves in the violent behaviour (e.g. Ann). The following quotations provide examples of these turning points in the narratives of Frances and Ann:

> **Frances:** He said, I'm going to come back in the night and I'm going to burn this house with you and your children in the bed. And it was actually when he threatened to do that to the children that I said, no more, I'm not putting up with it.

> **Ann:** I was standing by the window, and he [son] came towards me and he punched me in the chest, and he punched me with such force that I fell back against the window and it broke… I think it was about two weeks later I walked out, and I never went back again.

For Susan, the escalation of abuse to include physical violence prompted her to seek external help for a permanent end to the relationship, while for Liz, Margaret and Phil, the turning point could be said to be the realisation that the abuse would not end and they themselves would have to end the relationship. In Liz's and Phil's case, this realisation was more slow burning and had occurred some time previously, but the help that had been sought up to that point, from external systems, was not effective. For them it was the eventual intervention of appropriate (or in Phil's case, unorthodox) advice and help that enabled them to find permanent safety.

> **Liz:** And I said I've had enough. Enough is enough, I can't take it. I knew I'd be in for something if I went home, so I ran down to the Garda Station at Kevin Street and I was in bits there, crying and in bits, and [the Garda] said, we'll make sure you get the help now. Don't go back to him. So they got me into [the Refuge].

> **Phil:** I couldn't get barring orders or annulment papers as I wasn't married to him. He wouldn't go. I was afraid to go near [social workers] because of the thing of not being married. I thought they'd take the kids off me. That's when one woman, and I won't say who, below in the county council, and the solicitor… They evicted the two of us. The letter from the solicitor, it wasn't really worth the paper it was written on, but he thought proceedings would follow… When he did go, I was chuffed… I was on a roll.

Ferraro and Johnson (1983) identified six 'catalysts' which prompt abused women to redefine their violent relationships and initiate an end to the relationship: (1) a change in the level of violence; (2) a change in resources; (3) a change in the relationship; (4) despair; (5) a change in the visibility of violence; and (6) external definitions of the relationship. Most of these catalysts for change can be identified in the narratives of the participants in this research. Susan and Frances for example, identify change in the level of violence as the turning point and catalyst for ending the relationship permanently, while for Margaret, it was the despair of realising that 'nothing had changed'.

The consequences of reaching a turning point which involved a radical reconstruction of the meaning of the relationship, and then taking specific steps to end the relationship, were, for all the women in this book that they finally left their abusive relationship and did not return.

Exit strategies

As the quotations from Phil's narrative above demonstrate, her story is an appropriate example of the use and/or usefulness of a variety of external systems by a young woman who was involved in a 15-year non-marital abusive relationship. Her story also illustrates themes discussed in the previous section of this chapter and Chapter 4.

Phil's story

Phil met her partner when she was in her mid-teens. They began a sexual relationship when she was 19 and she became pregnant when she was 23. From their early courtship, her narrative highlights the abusive control that was to escalate later into physical violence, but she constructed a positive meaning in which to reframe this control: 'Just possessive, but I was flattered by that. I thought he couldn't be away from me for a minute you know.' His reaction to the news of her pregnancy was not flattering however, as 'the first thing he turned around and said was "is it mine"?' Because Phil left Ireland at the time of her first pregnancy, her narrative recounts a great deal of reflection on the contemporary social and political context in which she lived and managed her life as the unmarried mother of two children. The Irish social context at the time of her pregnancy was 'the boat or Navan Road [Mother and Baby Home]'. Phil connects the public discourse surrounding unmarried motherhood at that time to her identity and subsequent decision making in relation to her partner: (the nuns in school) 'always said don't go with lots of men, and you're used baggage, and no man will have you, that was kind of in the back of me head.'

Displaying the self-confident agentic position which runs throughout the narrative, she found herself a small bedsitter, lived alone and delivered her first baby. This resistant and agentic response is clearly a very strong theme throughout her narrative, and is displayed in her reply to her partner after the birth of their child in England, while he was still in Ireland: 'I said I'd call her … I don't like that name he says. And I said tough, what have you ever done for her.' Her mother's illness resulted in her returning briefly to Ireland, where her meeting with her partner was not amicable. 'And I said, just get away from me! I'm home to see me mammy, I don't ever want to talk to you again.' She returned to England and resumed her life there, which was 'grand. I made friends there, I was told I'd get a house, a flat or something by the time [my daughter] would be one. And I was grand.'

Her partner came from Ireland to live with her, because as she learned later, he had stolen money from both his employer and his mother. Their life together began with escalating arguments, generally about money and homemaking arrangements, and the coming and going of her partner, back and forth to Ireland. She was working while he was often unemployed, and she described his expectation of her gender subject position as: 'Neanderthal.' 'Where's my breakfast?' 'And I'm going,' 'Have you two broken arms?' 'That's for a woman, what else would you be doing? That's what you should do.' Phil clearly did not accept this subject position without constant resistance.

Phil and her partner decided to have a second child, despite the advice of her midwife that she ought not to have a second child with a man who was an unreliable partner. 'Regardless, I just wanted a baby.' Phil had a secondary motive in wanting to have another child: 'I wanted to get married, but he wouldn't. I think, in the back of my mind I thought, that maybe if we had another baby, he would. God wasn't I an eejit!' The public stigma attached to unmarried motherhood was not restricted to Ireland at that time, and meshed with discriminatory stereotypes of the Irish in Britain. 'But you see, you get jibes from people, little remarks – is it because he's married to someone else? You see, there were a lot of Irishmen in England and they would tell the women they were living with, oh no we're split up, but we can't get a divorce because we're Irish.'

The first episode of physical violence recounted in her narrative occurred one evening when she had been socialising with friends from the street and she forgot her keys. When she knocked at the front door, 'He whipped the door open so quickly the weather board went flying up, and he grabbed me by the hair and threw me right across the hall. I went flying up in the air, hit against the kitchen door… 'where were you until now, who were you with?' I was grabbed again by the hair, pegged into the sitting room.' Phil's response to this episode was similar to the many other episodes of verbal and physical violence in her narrative: 'I thought he was a lunatic and I shouted something at him… I ran up the stairs, dived into the small bedroom and pulled the chest of drawers against the door, and threw the cot against it… I said, that is it, something inside me just died.' Phil also exercised her resistance by going to a refuge, but does not report finding it a very helpful experience at that time. The police were called on one occasion, but the combined experience of anti-Irish prejudice and the dismissal of domestic violence as a lesser crime, led to this being a less than helpful intervention: 'They came in, we were Irish, like the police would treat the Travellers here. Ah sure all you ever do is beat each other and drink. They didn't charge him, they didn't take him out, they just gave out to him there and then.'

Phil and her partner jointly decided to return to Ireland. She believed the relationship might work there, once the stress of anti-Irish prejudice was removed. This did not prove to be the case, and the verbal abuse, control and physical violence continued 'in waves'. Her partner then wanted to have a third child, and she did not. Once again, she found support for her resistance in her GP who colluded with her to pretend that 'it was in God's hands' even though he knew she was using the contraceptive pill. Phil's resistance and agentic strategising led her to return to night school and complete her Leaving Certificate.

As the violence continued, and her strength and self-confidence grew, she began making enquiries about her possible legal options. As the 1996 Domestic Violence Act had not at that time been enacted, she was unable to get a barring order as she was not married to her abusive partner. However, through the creativity of a number of individual professionals whom she approached (a policeman, a solicitor and a local authority official) she was able to make her partner believe that he would be arrested if he did not vacate the family home (of which she was the legal tenant). The policeman would 'take him out of the house and keep him locked up for the weekend. He did it three or four times.' When he received a letter from the solicitor advising him 'to vacate by a certain date and to cease to intimidate Phil and her two daughters' she was so afraid of his violent reaction that she left the family home and stayed with relatives. She went back only on the advice of the solicitor. The local authority then evicted the two of them, and allowed only Phil to return, leading him to believe that he would be arrested if he returned. Despite his pleas for a reconciliation, she refused as, 'I knew I'd never get him out again.' Phil continues to live alone. She continued her education and now has a Third Level qualification.

Patterns of help seeking

As Phil's story illustrates, the process of leaving is not usually a 'once off' event, but is rather a series of events and interventions entered into by the woman in collaboration with a range of external others. As with Phil, these may be at times helpful or at other times unhelpful or even clearly prejudicial.

Table 5.1 External systems used in the participants' exit strategies

Name	Family/ friends	Gardai	Refuge*	Counselling/ support group	Legal systems	Medical	Social worker
Ann	+++	+	+++	+	+		
Brenda	++	+++	+	+	+++		
Frances	++	++		+	++	+	+++
Liz		++	++++	++	+		
Lorraine	++					++	+
Margaret	+	+				++	
Phil	+			+++	+		
Rose	++	++		+++	++	+	
Sarah	+	+	++	+	+++	+	+
Susan	+		+	+	+	+	

*+Some, but not significant contact or involvement. ++Significant contact in the process of ending the violence. +++Very significant involvement in the process of ending the violence. *Includes use of transition and second stage housing.*

The narratives of all the other women summarised in these chapters, refer to contact with a range of what can be called 'external others', including family and friends, legal and police agencies, medical and social service personnel, housing and refuges, and voluntary agencies.

Table 5.1 provides a summary overview of these sources of external help sought by, or offered to, the women in the process of leaving the relationship in order to access safety.

As can be seen in Table 5.1, all of the women at some time encountered one or more official agency as a consequence of being in an abusive relationship. However, it should be noted that this summary does not represent the importance of the contacts with these systems that the women may have had at other times of their lives. For example, Sarah encountered the full gamut of available services, which included formal state agencies such as the police, the medical system (her GP, mental health services, child guidance clinic), the legal system, (free legal aid, private solicitors, district and family law court judges, court appointed psychologist), voluntary agencies such as Women's Aid and a refuge for women which included transitional housing, as well as informal support from a pastor and eventually from her siblings. Not all of these interventions were helpful or accessed to enable her to leave the relationship. Susan, on the other hand, encountered fewer of these services. The majority of the women, however, as can be seen, had been involved in more formal and informal sources of support and intervention, an experience which has been found in many other studies (Anderson and Saunders 2003; Watson and Parsons 2005).

The use of these resources by the women can be understood as resistance only when they were freely chosen by them in their search for safety and a non-violent relationship. Seeking out such help occurred at various times during the relationship. For example, Rose and Margaret sought counselling for themselves and their partners quite early on:

> **Rose:** My biggest problem then was getting [him] well. Because I saw him as an unwell man. You see? So we went, [he] went to a counsellor, and you know things got better for a while. That was after we'd been together for a year.
>
> **Margaret:** I said I have to do something about getting myself counselling.

Frances on the other could be said to 'have found herself' at the receiving end of external intervention rather than actively seeking it out for herself. This occurred as a result of her partner's hospitalisation in a local psychiatric hospital, and his 'disclosure' to the psychiatrist that she was abusing him. This put in action a series of events which resulted in the family being referred to the local social work department and the consequent assignment of both a social worker and a family support worker to the family. Frances's reaction to this uninvited, but ultimately welcome, official intervention, provides a helpful insight into involuntary interaction of abused women with external agencies. Frances describes this interaction with the social worker in a surprisingly amusing manner:

> **Frances:** I'd say it took me nearly two years to trust her. At first I used to call her Cruella de Ville! When I'd see the car coming, I'd say, God no, here's Cruella de Ville coming down the road in the car! Oh I hated her. I couldn't stand her at first.

Frances's initial dislike and distrust of the social worker must be understood from her standpoint and within the context of the wide-ranging abuse she was experiencing:

> **Frances:** And he said, 'Oh, it's all your fault.' And then he started blaming me. It's your fault the social worker's here. You told them in [the hospital] what I was like, and all. And if they take your kids, it's going to be your own fault. He used to be telling me, like, that's what [social worker] is coming for, to take the children. 'Oh she is only coming now for a couple of weeks, to see what you're like, and then she'll eventually take the kids from you.' So this made me hate [her].

In this extract, Frances's partner is actively reinforcing her fears that social workers' primary concern is to take children into care. His ability to undermine the social worker's role mirrors his abusive tactics in another respect – moving from verbal manipulation to threats of violence:

> **Frances:** Oh yea, he'd know she would be coming, like, and he'd say, 'Now if you say anything bad about me, now, you'll really be in for it when she's gone.' And I'd know I'd be in for it when she'd be gone… Oh, I lied and I lied.

Frances's partner's control of her interaction with the social worker was not, however, the only problematic element in this professional intervention. Once again the key to understanding this complex professional relationship lies in an understanding of Frances's own self-identity, and just as her partner's behaviour mirrors his abuse of her, her response mirrors her resistance to his abuse:

> **Frances:** So she knew then that I was just rebelling against her, she knew that. That I wouldn't listen to her, that it was up to myself. And I was going to take my own time... Yeah, like the Safety Order, now, I didn't want to get that. So she pushed me to getting that... And then I didn't use it... Because she knew that I'd been pushed into doing it, and I said, feck, I'm after getting a beating over it now, and I'm not going to use it.

This extract illustrates the manner in which Frances 'resists' the opposing coercive pressures which impinge on her freedom of action as a result of the involvement of the social work services, while she is still co-habiting with a violent man. As McGee (2000, p.126) points out, the involvement of social services while the woman is still living with her partner can lead to an increase in the violence she experiences, 'as the men perceive the involvement of social services as undermining their control of the women and children'. What the data in this book adds to this understanding of the unintended consequences of social work (or other professional) interventions, is that the woman may respond to them as she is responding to the abusive behaviour itself – that is in a manner which is congruent with her self-identity. Her responses are not random – they are part of the construction of her identity and her meaning making in these circumstances.

It does not, however, follow from this that only freely chosen interventions will ultimately be effective and welcome. Frances's ultimate assessment of the social worker, 'I really, really appreciate what she did for me and for the kids. I'm really, really thankful,' compares well with that of Brenda, who voluntarily went to see a counsellor (on the advice of her priest). 'She was there in body but not in mind. She was there and got switched off.' It is also interesting to note from these narratives that the provision (or imposition) of a social work service seems to be entirely dependent on chance. Frances was referred to the social work service only because her partner was assessed as extremely violent and his potential for lethal action was correctly diagnosed by an admitting psychiatrist, while Brenda, with three small children, whose partner was also potentially lethal (chasing her with a loaded shotgun and threatening to 'blow her brains out'), was also seen within the mental health services, but no action was taken nor referral made to any other service. The implication of this complex interaction between involvement with external systems, the nature of this involvement (i.e. whether voluntary or mandatory) and the woman's response to and utilisation of the system within her patterns of resistance and construction of identity and meaning, illustrate the difficulty of understanding women's journeys from abuse to safety from a linear or stages perspective (Chang *et al.* 2006).

Counselling and other support services

While it is clear from Table 5.1 that all of the women attended a support group and/or received individual counselling at some point in their journey to safety, it was only those groups or counsellors who were specifically focused on or experienced in working with abused women who were identified by them as 'extremely helpful'.

> **Liz:** V [support worker in Refuge] was brilliant to me.

> **Rose:** I was very afraid of going… I suppose it was like an alcoholic going to an AA meeting, an admission that you had a problem. And I went, and it was just wonderful! They gave me more than I could ever have hoped.

It is also clear that these specialised counselling/support services, together with the organisations such as local refuges or Women's Aid, are the most helpful of the interventions from the women's standpoint. Only Brenda (as noted on p.89) reported dissatisfaction with the counselling she received. This supports the work of Moe (2007) and Goodman *et al.* (2003) who both found that the intervention rated most helpful by the study participants was contact with a specialised domestic violence programme. Many of the women in this book availed of refuge and/or transition housing services, and these were also evaluated by them as extremely helpful. Moe (2007, p.679) also found that services and refuges that are flexible and provide women with the assistance they need, including continuous and longer-term support, 'report higher success rates in terms of recipient satisfaction and long-term independence.' Only Margaret, Lorraine and Susan did not have the involvement of the police in their final exit strategies (though Lorraine had considerable indirect contact with them because of her partner's criminal background). Of the remaining women, only Sarah expressed dissatisfaction with both the support of the police and the legal systems with which she came into contact – examples of the 'institutional failures' that Moe (2007) refers to.

> **Sarah:** He [solicitor] wasn't very nice actually. When I went to him initially, he sarcastically said, well you left your home, why do you want to go back? A smirk on his face.

As Goodkind *et al.* (2003, p.349) note, even though there is extensive recent research which has documented battered women's multiple coping strategies and logical decision making in order to keep themselves and their families safe, 'this expertise is still not recognised by many people or by society.' Sarah's experience with the legal system would certainly support this contention.

Role of family members/friends

Table 5.1 also shows that while the women utilised a wide range of professional and voluntary services, in almost all cases, they also received support and help at various stages of their journey through and out of the violence from family and friends.

> **Rose:** So I rang my mother and broke down on the phone, and she said, pack a bag and bring the boys home… So then when I came home, my mother rang him and told him to move out of the house.

This is consistent with other research in this field (Goodkind *et al.* 2003; Moe 2007). Reviewing this research, Goodkind *et al.* (2003, p.348) concluded that, 'Battered women seek help from family and friends for advice, inspiration, and encouragement, but also for tangible support.'

These data suggest that the decision making in which the woman engages at this point in her journey cannot be fully understood without reference to her perceptions of the meaning of the abuse and her relationship, and to her strategies of resistance. All the elements of the journey now coalesce in a pattern which is different from the previous patterns: her constructions of the meaning and effects of the abuse; her perceptions of the consequences of this abuse for both her physical safety and her identity as a woman, a partner and a mother; and the availability of an effective source of outside support which acts as the catalyst in a manner which can be compared to a cook adding yeast when making bread. The yeast may or may not have been available to the woman at an earlier point within the wider social environment, but if the other ingredients have not been gathered, she will not reach for it, or avail of its presence, as Rose's comment suggests: 'I could have walked away very early on. I'm not saying I should have, because I didn't.' On the other hand, if the other ingredients have been gathered, and the support is not available to her, because of what Moe (2007) calls 'institutional failures', she cannot complete the task, and will be forced to delay ending the relationship, a delay which may result in serious and life-threatening injury: ('He'd blow my brains out' – Brenda). Or it may result in lethal self-harm (as some of the women hinted in these interviews, e.g. 'Having suicidal thoughts, and just my whole life falling down around me' – Rose).

Critical turning points: 'no going back'

The 'ubiquitous' nature (Coates and Wade 2004) of the women's strategies of resistance was explored in detail in Chapter 3. The ultimate act of resistance for the women in this book, though not for all women (Anderson and Saunders 2003; Peled *et al.* 2000), was finally leaving the abusive relationship and ending their intimate involvement with their abusive partner. The manner of this final rupture was unique and idiosyncratic for all the women. These are the critical points of rupture (which can also be titled 'critical turning points').

Brenda's narrative describes her process of leaving and the difficulties she experienced in finally rupturing the marital relationship. Like the women in Moe's (2007) study, Brenda also 'utilised a myriad of helping', including a Women's Refuge, a priest, a counsellor and the Gardai on a number of occasions. However, she identifies one particular visit to the Garda Station as the intervention which finally enabled her to take the steps to seek safety:

> **Brenda:** Because he [husband] worked as a kind of bouncer in the area the odd night, he knew the Guards. The older Guards. It was only when the two new guys who came to the area, they were after coming out of Dublin and they were after dealing with cases like this – seeing it – and they knew straight away. And only for them, I tell you the truth – that was it.

Liz's narrative of leaving is somewhat similar, as she too had been to a number of women's hostels (but not refuges) on the previous occasions when she left her husband. It was the intervention of a young Garda on duty in the station to which she ran who directed her to the appropriate Women's Refuge, which enabled her to eventually separate permanently. In these two cases it is clear that appropriate support and information by the Gardai were the facilitative factors which made the final rupture possible. This reflects the findings of McGee's study (2000) in which the respondents valued police responses that were timely, that took the issue of domestic violence seriously, and made appropriate referrals to other agencies including refuges, solicitors and support groups. Brenda's initial lack of support from the Gardai reflects Moe's (2007, p.686) study in which many women reported that 'calling the police did not improve their situation'.

However, Liz's and Brenda's experiences can be contrasted with the other narratives which follow a somewhat different pattern, thereby raising an issue which needs to be explored. While all of the women had contact with a range of agencies, and all described an event which can be identified as 'the point of no return' (and these are identified in each woman's story), there is clearly a time for each woman when a confluence of factors – including fear, exhaustion, increasing danger and availability of appropriate information and support – come together to enable her to take that definitive step away from the relationship. For Brenda the arrival of new Gardai in the local station appears to have been the critical factor which enabled her to take the definitive step to leave.

For Margaret it was the sudden and certain realisation that things would never change:

> **Margaret:** That broke the camel's back... He hadn't changed. There was nothing about his manner, the way he looked at me, the way he spoke to me. Nothing had changed... that night I knew that was it. Like I couldn't live the rest of my life, living this seesaw of a relationship, because it was doing my head in. The happy family syndrome was doing my head in because I wasn't happy. It wasn't a happy marriage.

What can be seen in these examples is another essential step in the journeys to safety which ended the relationship. While Rose had previously sought various forms of help to attempt to ameliorate the abuse and make her marriage work, Margaret only sought help *after* a final defining episode of violence and when she realised that things would not change:

> **Margaret:** Because I know when I started to go and get help (from WOVE and my doctor)... I started to realise that it wasn't me, me, me all the time. You know it wasn't me that was going mad.

A new model of analysis

Dutton (1996, p.105) suggests that 'we need to understand better what explains the differences in strategic responses among battered women'. These data provide an insight into these differences in responses by highlighting the intricate interrelationship between self-identity, meaning reconstruction and resistance in the women's narratives. The highly individualistic and context specific nature of this interrelationship contributes to the extreme difficulty which outsiders, whether family, friends or professionals, may have in understanding the processes by which abused women negotiate the journey from abuse to safety. These findings suggest that an understanding of the dynamic interrelationship between these three aspects of the women's narratives is a necessary and helpful guide in assisting such an understanding of this dangerous and unique process. Figure 5.1 represents these three concepts in diagrammatic format.

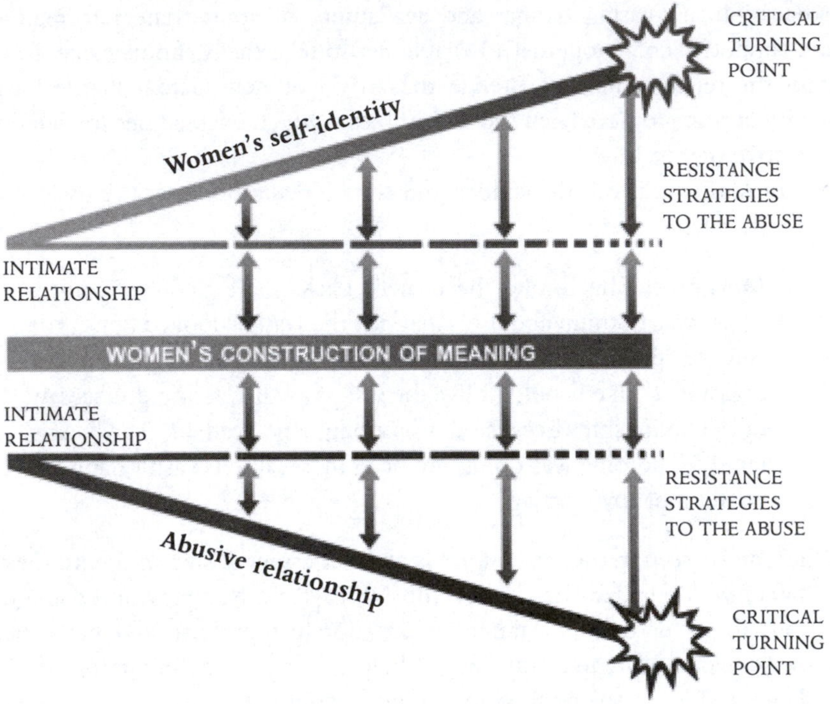

Figure 5.1 Identity, meaning, resistance and abuse: A new model of analysis

The data suggest that each woman will approach her intimate relationship with a unique self-identity. This is represented by the upper line in the diagram. It is important to stress that this self-identity is not in any way indicative of, nor contributes to, the abusive relationship in which she finds herself. The abuse is an independent choice of behaviours by her partner, and is therefore not dependent on her identity. In making and maintaining an intimate relationship with her partner, the woman constructs meaning for the relationship which is congruent with her identity, her affection for her partner and her hopes and expectations for the future. This intimate relationship or 'marital project' is represented by the broken lower line, and the meaning she constructs for this relationship is represented by the middle line. This could be seen when some of the women reconstructed the warning signals, which were apparent to others at the beginning of the relationship, in a manner which was congruent with their own meaning construction. This construction may, as for example in the case of Rose, involve agentic resistance to the wishes of those (her parents) whose meanings and attributions are in conflict with her own meaning and identity. These meanings are also influenced by the public discourses and romance narratives (Kulkarni 2007; Wood 2001) with which the wider society circumscribes both gender identity and gender relationships. As Neimeyer (2000a, p.264) notes: 'Individuals make meaning by drawing selectively on a fund of discourses that precedes them and that is consensually validated within their cultures, subcultures, communities and families.'

The lower line represents the abusive behaviours, and the broken line represents the marital project as it changes and disintegrates as a result of this abuse. However, once the relationship is established and the escalation of abusive behaviours becomes apparent (lower line), the woman engages in the range of resistant behaviours which were discussed above. This resistance can have one or more of three possible outcomes: (1) to change (end) the abusive behaviour; (2) to change (i.e. reconstruct) the meaning the woman attributes to the relationship and to the abuse; and/or (3) to change the woman's own self-identity in a way which reduces the growing dissonance between this identity and her abusive experiences. All three of these outcomes are evident in the analysis of the narratives which has been discussed above. These resistant responses are represented by the vertical arrows. They are positioned between the upper and lower lines and the middle line, as they represent the woman's attempts to both withstand the violence and reduce the dissonance between her preferred identity as a loved and 'normal' wife/partner/mother, and the reality of her abusive relationship. As Moe (2007, p.684) suggests, 'Most of the women's help-seeking efforts occurred during their abusive relationships as they attempted to prevent further assaults and salvage their relationships.' Resistance now takes on a 'double level of intentionality' – i.e. to both reduce or eliminate the abuse and maintain acceptable levels of safety, and also to contribute to the reconstruction of meaning and (to a more limited extent) the redefinition of identity.

Conclusion

Coates and Wade's (2004) contention that resistance is ubiquitous can now be understood within this context of meaning construction. When these resistant behaviours are viewed in the context of women's constant reconstruction of meaning in order to reduce the dissonance between their identity and their experiences, these behaviours take on a completely new appearance, they become a journey to coherence of meaning, identity and experience. The following two chapters will outline how narrative therapy can assist professionals working with women experiencing such abuse to hear these complexities and support them to make decisions to keep themselves safe.

Chapter 6

Narrative Therapy in Working with Abused Women

In view of Wade's (2007) observation that response-based therapy which seeks to highlight resistance and agency uses systemic, narrative and feminist therapeutic approaches, this chapter will review and discuss the development and principal elements of narrative and collaborative therapy in social work and counselling. While all narrative approaches are based within a postmodern approach to therapeutic interventions, different authors emphasise different aspects of this contemporary way of working with both women and men.

Narrative therapies

It is perhaps more accurate to refer to narrative 'therapies' in the plural, as they are a developing approach to working with people in distress who seek therapeutic help (Abels and Abels 2001; Brown and Augusta-Scott 2007). These narrative therapies are part of what Anderson (1997) calls the 'paradigmatic' shift to postmodern psychotherapy. They have their roots in the interdisciplinary (including social work) modernist theoretical approaches to family therapy, but have moved from the earlier conceptualisations of family systems functioning, with their emphases on 'hierarchy and patriarchy' through the 'second-order' 'observing and evolutionary systems' to an awareness of the role of language and a postmodern social constructionist paradigm (Anderson 1997). They have their epistemological roots in the sociological theories of Foucault (1980, 1981, 1989) and Goffman (1961, 1974), and in Bruner's (1986, 1990) and Bateson's (1972, 1979) studies of linguistics, text and meaning. The similarity of approaches within these narrative therapies, however, can tend to disguise their subtle differences of emphases.

The influence of Michael White

Amongst the many contributors to what can be described as this 'wide church' of narrative therapy, the names of Michael White (1989, 1995, 2000, 2007) and David Epston (1990 with Michael White) are cited by many writers as key contributors to the development of narrative approaches in therapy and social work. It will therefore be helpful to highlight some of their principal therapeutic concepts and techniques before discussing other approaches to narrative counselling and therapy.

White identifies the work of Michel Foucault (1980, 1995), particularly his theories of power/knowledge, the subjugation of naïve knowledges, and the concepts of the 'normalising gaze'(i.e. the overall public gaze which controls our actions) and 'docile bodies' as being strongly influential in his development of narrative therapy (White and Epston 1990). Drawing on these concepts, White, and others writing in this postmodern paradigm, reject the earlier structural systemic approaches to therapeutic intervention which sees 'some underlying structure or dysfunction' in the family as leading to the behaviour of individuals in the family, adopting instead an 'interpretive' method which proposes that it is the meanings that individuals contribute to their life events that determine behaviour. White draws on the work of Bateson (1972, 1979) and Goffman (1974) for this concept of an 'interpretive' rather than a 'linear' understanding of causality. Similarly, Anderson (1997) suggests that postmodern influences on psychotherapy, including on her own 'collaborative' therapy, utilise an interpretive perspective which emphasises constructed rather than imposed meaning.

The narrative metaphor

Bruner's (1986) understanding of stories influenced White's use of the text analogy to describe the centrality of 'stories' in individuals' efforts to comprehend the events of their lives:

> In striving to make sense of their lives, persons face the task of arranging their experiences of events in sequences across time in such a way as to arrive at a coherent account of themselves and the world around them. (White and Epston 1990, p.10)

Narrative, when used in this sense (as distinct from the literary sense), is a storytelling metaphor of the way we 'compose our lives' (Anderson 1997). These stories or 'self-narratives' have ' emotional resonance', impacting not only on people's actions and attitudes, but also on their 'sense of identity'. They must have a beginning (i.e. history), a middle (i.e. present) and an end (i.e. a future), and can therefore be future-determined as well as past-determined (White and Epston 1990). In recounting these self-narratives, individuals often recount them in what White calls 'problem saturated talk' (pp.10–12), which gives life and support to the problem and the individual's or family's relationship with the problem. Stories are not merely a recounting of reality, they are themselves constitutive of reality.

'Externalising the problem'

White suggests that one of the tasks of the therapist is to search for 'unique outcomes' (White 2007, p.232) to the dominant story, outcomes which may not be heard in the problem as storied by the individual or by others. Drawing on the work of Foucault (1980), White (2007, p.232) suggests that dominant stories reflect the power/knowledge relationship, whereby 'global' and 'unitary' knowledges, i.e. those seen and accepted as objective 'truth', subjugate local or 'naïve' knowledges. White's development of the technique of 'externalising the problem' (p.26) facilitates the exploration of these subjected voices and knowledges, as well as the identification of unique outcomes.

Externalising a problem enables it to be objectified and opens up its various components to analysis, separating the problem from the impact of its power in the individual's life (Miller 2006). This separation also facilitates the recognition of both the subjugated and dominant knowledge in the story (Brown 2007). Externalising conversations permit different ways of speaking about the problem to be heard (White 2007). Externalisation, therefore, facilitates the identification and valorisation of resistance to abuse and power. Appropriate questions can elicit accounts of 'defiance' and refusal to perform according to expectations, and can also invite speculation about other possibilities for resistance in a woman's life.

Risks of externalisation

In the context of violence and abuse, however, the technique of externalisation needs to be handled with particular care. The most commonly known example of such 'externalisation' is the case study known as 'Sneaky Poo' in which a six-year-old boy and his family attend therapy for his encopresis (faecal incontinence) (White and Epston 1990). The externalising and naming of the problem as 'Sneaky Poo' suggests a somewhat light-hearted and 'less stressed' approach to the problem (White and Epston 1990), which may have been appropriate with a six-year-old child. Carr (2002) questions the appropriateness of using narrative approaches in certain circumstances, referring to the ethical implications of using them where there are threats to clients' safety. White himself notes, however, that therapists must always be conscious of the 'local' politics of each relationship and must never, inadvertently, contribute to an individual's oppression in a relationship. Consequently, problems and experiences such as violence and abuse must never be externalised, but the attitudes and beliefs that underpin the violence, and the strategies that maintain the abuse, such as secrecy and isolation, can safely be externalised. Miller (2006) discusses this dilemma with specific reference to social work practice, suggesting that externalisation is unhelpful in a crisis situation, and should not be introduced until the immediate crisis and risk have passed. She also emphasises that responsibility for harm caused to others must not be minimised by the use of these techniques.

'Recruiting an audience'

White (1995, 2007) and White and Epston (1990) have emphasised the importance of 'recruiting an audience' to witness to and authenticate the preferred stories of individuals in therapy. They use a range of techniques, including letters of invitation, awards and certificates, to involve this potential audience in what White (based on Myerhoff 1982) describes as 'definitional ceremonies' (White and Epston 1990, p.49). This enables the involvement of an audience who may or may not be actually physically present (or even still alive) to contribute to the consolidation of preferred identities and new meanings, as well as to the revision of previous meanings.

Therapy as colonisation

Narrative approaches to therapy and counselling reject the 'pathologising' power of expert knowledge and judgements and emphasise collaborative assessments of the causes of people's distress. Anderson (1997, 2007) specifically titles her work 'collaborative therapy'. Not all writers, however, unquestioningly accept this benign understanding of therapy and counselling. Kitzinger for example (1993) queries the value of any form of therapy to women or to feminism. She sees no need to distinguish between diverse theoretical approaches to therapy, interrogating the very possibility that any form of therapy can make the 'personal political' and coming to the unequivocal conclusion that 'feminism and psychology are not ethically or politically compatible' (p.496). In a plenary paper on Family Therapy and Social Justice presented to a Family Therapy Conference in Melbourne, Kiwi

Tamasese (Waldegrave and Tamasese 1994, p.204) reflected powerfully on the colonising practices of therapy without sensitivity to its political and relational contexts:

> I think of colonisation, no longer with the might of the sword, no longer with the decimation through disease, but through the gentle conversation of a therapist assuming the rightness of her/his value system, or, more dangerously, assuming that the discipline is scientific, therefore value free, therefore intercultural and international.

As McCarthy (1995, p.171), however, notes, '"the personal is always political" in working with those who are at the margins in society.' She suggests that therapists cannot be blind to the issues of power and justice in clinical work and in what she describes as the 'colonising' practices of service delivery in such work. McCarthy (1997) and Salamon (1994) suggest 'participatory ethics' as a means of recognising and deconstructing the power of dominant discourses in therapeutic and social service contexts. This demands recognition by the therapist that they do not listen from a 'neutral position', and consequently demands a therapeutic orientation which privileges the client's voice and story (McCarthy 1997).

Swan (1999) counters arguments such as Kitzinger's (1993) from a narrative therapeutic perspective, which takes Foucault's 'power as lived' understanding of power as constituted and exercised at a local level. She argues that these approaches can expose and 'localise discourse for discussion and contestation, bringing light to previously obscured ideas which trap women and have us blame ourselves for our problems' (p.111). Emphasis on structural mechanisms of power limits political action to large-scale macro-level activity, and thereby misses the pervasive day-to-day local level methods of control and oppression, a point which was also made by McCarthy (1997).

'Not knowing'?

Anderson (1997, 2007) addresses this dilemma of the power imbalance between therapist and client by adopting a 'not knowing stance'. For Anderson this means that therapists must listen in such a way that their previous experience does not prevent them from hearing the full meaning of the client's description of their experience. This can only happen if the therapist approaches each clinical experience from the position of 'not knowing'. This also implies that roles are reversed and the 'client becomes the teacher'. Brown (2007, p.9), however, takes issue with what she describes as this 'potentially dangerous "relativism"' which treats all stories as equal. While acknowledging that Anderson does not call herself a narrative therapist, she suggests that she uses the narrative metaphor, and her 'not knowing' position has influenced narrative therapists in a manner that is relativist and reifies personal experience. Brown argues that in many situations (such as violence and abuse), one must take a position, because, 'anything does not go' (Brown 2007, p.9). She suggests that the values of the collaborative postmodern therapeutic approach (such as Anderson's) must be 'blended' with a modernist vision of social justice, which recognises the oppressive nature of dominant discourses and challenges these discourses.

Brown's (2007) suggestion mirrors that of Fraser and Nicholson (1990) regarding the necessity of valuing postmodern contributions to feminist theory while not abandoning objectivity, and the 'synthetic' approach to the understanding of domestic violence advocated by Dobash *et al.* (2007) and Heise's (1998) 'nested ecological' model. These approaches suggest that individual level factors, which would include individual constructions of meanings and individual choices, co-exist with (and within) cultural discourses and consequently within wider social structures. Such an approach contributes to the development of a 'politicised practice' of the kind which is presented in this book.

These perspectives on the collaborative or 'not knowing' emphases in narrative approaches are particularly relevant in the context of the exercise of power and control in the lives of abused women, opening up possibilities for 'political' (with a small 'p') action and recognition of their resistance not only within their intimate relationships, but within social work relationships and interventions (Abels and Abels 2001).

The contributions of narrative approaches to diversity and violence

The sensitivity to power relations in both the therapeutic relationship (as discussed above) and in the wider social context is one of the important contributions of collaborative and narrative approaches. These influences have been explicitly formularised, for example, in a diverse range of therapeutic and community interventions and approaches to intimate partner violence. Jenkins (1990) for example, has written consistently on his work with sexual and domestic violence offenders. Gray (2007) has utilised White's concept of the 'migration of identity' to facilitate violent men to deconstruct dominant beliefs that support male violence. Tamasese (2007) reflects on the intersection of gender and culture and the development of the 'Stop Abuse' community project in Samoa to combat violence against women in a culturally sensitive manner. These works are amongst many examples of the influence of narrative ideas, which foreground political, gender and cultural sensitivity, in developing responses to intimate partner violence that go beyond the one to one therapeutic intervention.

Narrative Process Theory

As noted in the previous section, narrative approaches are not a unitary phenomenon but are rather a family of therapeutic approaches whose influence on counselling and therapy is growing, and which are consequently themselves undergoing continual development (Payne 2007). One such development is found in the work of Angus and colleagues (Angus *et al.* 1999, p.1256) who describe their approach as the Narrative Process Theory of therapy (Angus *et al.* 1999). The philosophical approach underpinning this theory or model of narrative therapy is indistinguishable from that of White and Epston or Anderson, as it is predicated on the assumption that successful psychotherapy entails the 'articulation, elaboration, and transformation of the client's self-told story or macronarrative.'

Angus and her colleagues outline three distinct modes of inquiry within the therapeutic process: (1) The external narrative mode, which involves the description and elaboration of life events in which the story of 'what happened' is addressed; (2) The internal narrative mode, which involves the exploration and elaboration of subjective feelings, reactions and emotions related to the life events; and (3) The reflexive narrative mode, which explores the meaning of both what happened and the emotions relating to it. The purpose of these processes is to develop a new understanding of 'what happened' which either supports or challenges the implicit beliefs which underpin the dominant narrative. According to Angus *et al.* (1999), this exploration of the subjective experience of events provides both worker and client with a 'rich spawning ground for the creation of new meanings' (p.1257). This meaning making is facilitated by the exploration of personal expectations, needs and motivations, anticipations and beliefs of both the individual and those individuals who play significant roles in the client's life.

Angus *et al.*'s (1999) emphasis on meaning making within the narrative therapeutic paradigm reflects the influence of Bateson (1979) on the interpretive stance within narrative. This accepts that people perceive their experiences within their own preconceived frameworks, and must 'interpret' (i.e. 'make sense') of new ideas within these existing beliefs and assumptions.

The narrative approach of Robert Neimeyer

Neimeyer (1995a), coming from a more explicitly constructivist stance, places even greater emphasis on the role of the construction and reconstruction of meaning as individuals narrate the events of their lives. At the core of Neimeyer's constructivist approach is 'the belief that people give meaning to their experiences by using a storytelling structure.' He believes that the function of these narratives is 'to establish continuity of meaning in the client's lived experience' (Neimeyer 1995d, p.233). Neimeyer's work is influenced by what he describes as the 'groundbreaking' personal construct theory of George Kelly (1955). He summarises constructivism as viewing human beings as inveterate meaning makers, constructing their involvement in the world in ways that express their own particular cultures, families and individual personalities (Neimeyer 2000b).

As has been noted above, narrative approaches to social work and therapy are not a 'homogenous field'. Approaches differ epistemologically in their particular blend of modern and postmodern conceptualisations and practices (Brown and Augusta-Scott 2007). Neimeyer's therapeutic approach has grown explicitly out of a synthesis of social constructionism and constructivism, incorporating postmodern understandings of identity as a fluid, non-essentialist, socially constructed 'saturated self' (Gergen 1991) together with a contingent symbolic view of language as merely arbitrary 'signifiers' of meaning (Neimeyer 1998). He summarises this synthesis as follows: 'Social constructionism can interject into the practice of constructivist counselling a heightened awareness of the rhetorical nuances and implications of both the client's and therapist's discourse, as well as greater sensitivity to the broader cultural, institutional and power arrangements in which counsellors inevitably work' (1998, p.140). This suggests that the meanings to an experience attached by the individual must be heard clearly by the therapist. This passage also hints at Neimeyer's awareness of the role of the therapist's power and the power of discursive professional practices.

Therapeutic approach

Starting from this philosophical (and political) stance, Neimeyer utilises the Narrative Process Model (NPM) of Angus *et al.* (1999) to develop his own therapeutic intervention approach. To this narrative process he adds a 'narrative structure' which includes setting, characterisation, plot, theme and fictional goal (Neimeyer and Levitt 2001). The setting establishes the context of the story, the 'where and when' of the event(s). The characterisation refers to the 'who' of the story, the subjective worlds of the storyteller, and the other supporting characters. The plot is, as one would expect, the storyline of the events which fit together into a coherent account. The theme is the 'why', which provides a deeper level meaning which is often implicit and inferred. The fictional goal refers to the 'why' behind the plot. This is a term which is open to misunderstanding as it does not mean that the goal of the plot is untrue or imaginary. The term is drawn from the constructivist view and means that the self-narrative is 'fashioned or invented by the narrator' (Neimeyer and Levitt 2001).

Heuristic and healing

In discussing the value of this specific narrative approach to coping with trauma, Neimeyer and Levitt (2001) draw attention to the distinction between micronarratives and macronarratives, suggesting that the production of a macronarrative that draws attention to, and highlights, an individual's coping patterns and strategies is important in the treatment of traumatised individuals. One way to do this is by reflecting on the many micronarratives that involve successful coping with adversity, and from these to establish a macronarrative, or 'preferred story' which anchors the individual's identity in particular and specific aspects of their lives. The reflexive narrative (Angus *et al.* 1999) also enables one to reflect on one's experiences and responses to adversity, permitting us to perceive our behaviour as, for example, resistance, and thus to construct an identity for ourselves as 'copers' (Neimeyer and Levitt 2001). Such an approach to professional interventions with abused women reflects the work of Wade (1997, 2000, 2007), as well as that of White (1995) and White and Epston (1990).

Therapeutic engagement

Neimeyer (1995c) sets out a number of elements in the counselling and therapy relationship which enable the individual to face the challenges of reconstructing long-standing narratives of meaning and identity. The most relevant of these for social work and counselling intervention with women experiencing abuse are summarised in Table 6.1.

Table 6.1 Strategic and technique preferences of constructivist approaches

Area	Strategic preferences	Intervention techniques
Assessment focus	Exploration of personal narratives, personal and family constructs.	Identification of central metaphors, life reviews.
Goal of intervention	Promotion of meaning making.	Facilitation of meaningful accounts.
Style of therapy	Empathetic grasping of client's outlook.	'Credulous'/'not knowing' approach.
Approach to resistance*	Understood as legitimate protection of core-ordering processes.	Externalising the problem, identification of unique outcomes.

Adapted from Neimeyer (1995b, p.17)
**'Resistance' in this sense is the limited therapeutic use of the word rejected by Wade (1997) and discussed earlier in Chapter 3.*

Neimeyer has developed a range of therapeutic techniques which can support distressed individuals in the disturbing challenge of rebuilding their world in the face of trauma and loss (Neimeyer 1995c, 2000b). Amongst these techniques, the following would be suitable for working with abused women:

- *Biographies*: a written record that provides an account of the significant events, persons, places and projects that shaped the individual's life.
- *Casual enactments*: brief, informal role-plays designed to enable the individual to experiment with a particular part or role. These can also be non-verbal.
- *Drawing and painting*: symbolic drawings and artistic expressions can be interrogated for their nuances of meaning.
- *Journals*: written narratives can enable individuals to confront and explore choices in relationships, place past traumas in a contemporary frame of reference and give 'voice' to unexpressed hopes.
- *Loss characterisations*: open-ended instructional prompts at the top of blank paper which gives an individual the opportunity to respond

as they see fit, and which can then be interrogated for meaning in more formal ways.

- *Personal pilgrimage*: to re-establish connections with persons, places and traditions that have grown distant or disconnected from current lives.

This last technique would seem to be particularly appropriate for work with abused women for whom isolation from friends and family is a common form of control and abuse (Dobash and Dobash 1998; Kirkwood 1993).

Constructivist or constructionist?

As discussed earlier in this chapter, narrative approaches are a wide, but not homogenous field. Most fundamentally, there are differences in epistemological foundations and influences. In view of these differing perspectives, Neimeyer, as discussed above, proposes a synthesis of constructivist and social constructionist therapeutic approaches. Neimeyer (1995a) acknowledges the influence of George Kelly (1955), the 'central name in constructivism' on his work. Kelly's *The Psychology of Personal Constructs* (1955) focuses attention on an individual's personal meaning making process, what he terms 'his personal constructs' (Kelly 1955, 1963), while social constructionism, as was discussed above, focuses on discourse and language in the construction of meaning and reality. Anderson (1997) places constructivism in the 'second order cybernetics' phase of the evolution of family therapy, and therefore in a modernist epistemological paradigm. On the other hand, both can be placed in the 'anti-objectivist' stance of postmodernism and can be distinguished by suggesting that constructivism focuses on individual cognitive processes, while constructionism focuses on the communicative process, including the use of language, within and between people. The resulting debates between constructionists and constructivists have therefore centred on personal/social (or cognitive/performative) differences in emphasis (McNamee 2004). Kelly, however, in his 'Sociality Corollary' (1963) moved himself into what McNamee (2004) calls 'the relational realm to explore the human activity of meaning making'. Neimeyer (2000b) also identifies the intra-interpersonal distinction as a means of bridging the constructivist and constructionist positions. In reflecting on the relationship between constructivism and constructionism, McNamee (2004) suggests that constructivists like Neimeyer have utilised and amplified the relational aspects of Kelly's constructivism, allowing the 'residual individualism' to recede into the background.

Raskin, Weihs and Morano (2005, p.14) suggest that it is more appropriate to refer to 'constructivisms' because there are 'many varieties of constructivisms'. From this broader perspective, Raskin (2005, p.2) places 'social constructionism' within the constructivist field, as it 'centres on meaning making as psychology's primary focus of inquiry'.

Despite the differing emphases, starting points and terminology, constructivists and social constructionists share a common desire to engage in transformative dialogue, and social and personal change (McNamee 2004). In this manner they could be said to be keeping faith with Kelly's (1963, p.44) hopes for a 'good theory', in that it should be 'fertile in producing new ideas, in generating hypotheses, in provoking experimentation, in encouraging inventions'.

Narrative social work in the context of abuse

Drawing on these approaches to, and interpretations of, narrative therapy and counselling, Wood and Roche (2001) and Roche and Wood (2005) explore the value of deconstructive narrative-based models of intervention. In their 2001 paper, 'An emancipatory principle for social work with survivors of male violence', Wood and Roche note the need to 'repoliticise' interventions with abused women, which they claim has seen the theoretical base of such work overtaken by 'medical–psychological' approaches. Working from the premise of 'internalised oppression', they adapt the narrative approach of White (1989, 1995) and White and Epston (1990), to propose four transformative processes on which to base their model of intervention: (a) externalising; (b) deconstructive questioning; (c) seeking resistance–defiance; and (d) anchoring.

Transformative processes

The concept of 'externalising', is a widely accepted narrative therapy technique which separates the person from the problem. Rather than referring to the client's depression, the worker refers to '*the depression*' (Wood and Roche 2001, p.72). The risks involved in using externalising in the context of violence and abuse have been discussed earlier in this chapter. 'Deconstructive questioning' moves the narrative to a more political level, and helps the survivor to connect her personal experiences to wider cultural beliefs about women. These questions are informed by postmodern critiques of discourses, which identify and query the dominance of such discourses at both the personal and political levels. As Wood and Roche note, such awareness raising about the relationship of micro-level intimate abuse and wider oppressive cultural and gender discourses, enables women to free themselves from self-blame and may even encourage them to become involved at a more collective level in challenging such discourses and behaviours. They name the third process as 'seeking resistance and defiance' (p.74). Their outline of this process resembles very closely the work of Alan Wade (1997, 2000, 2007), which has been discussed above. They affirm strongly that 'women *do* resist', and that 'this resistance takes many forms' (p.76). Their suggestion, however, that 'searching for remembered moments... which foreshadow new stories of who the survivor is' (p.76) link the concept of resistance with that of identity, which is the explicit purpose of the fourth process of this model. 'Anchoring' embeds the resistance of the present experience in the past. It suggests that the woman's current behaviour is rooted to some extent in her behaviour in the past. This concept resonates with Neimeyer and Levitt's (2001) macronarratives of resilience and coping.

In a later paper, Roche and Wood (2005) again suggest that their model of working with survivors of abuse starts from the need to counteract and challenge the pervasive 'woman blaming' that surrounds male violence against women, which they say is expressed by both perpetrators and those who purport to assist women. Their amended model, which they claim now contains three narrative processes for feminist social work, enables women to 'co-construct new identity stories' (p.466) for themselves. They base their understanding of identity and resistance on the social constructionism of Berger and Luckmann (1967) and suggest that the necessary social work and counselling processes must also understand and engage identity as mutable and socially produced. They propose three interrelated processes in order to do this: (a) seeking resistance; (b) anchoring resistance; and (c) elaborating new stories. Seeking resistance in this model more closely resembles Wade's (1997, 2000, 2007) approach as it involves 'focused listening'.

Conclusion

The literature discussed above suggests that the narrative therapeutic approaches for counselling and social work developed by Neimeyer and his colleagues, influenced by the work of White and Epston, are particularly relevant for working with survivors of trauma and abuse. The aim of these approaches is to utilise procedures for developing life narratives that can accommodate traumatic experiences (Neimeyer 2000b), within a context of resilience, coping and resistance. As has been noted above, these approaches are part of a growing trend in social work and counselling towards the incorporation of constructivist (Fook 2002), constructionist (Abels and Abels

2001; Parton and O'Byrne 2000) and narrative approaches to individual and family work (Payne 2007). What Neimeyer and Levitt (2001, p.64) call the 'ubiquity' of storytelling in our everyday lives, has become a tool for the organisation of individuals' responses to trauma and abuse. Narrative can therefore be both healing and heuristic, enabling the individual her/himself to be the author of an idiosyncratic macro self-narrative which is marked by resilience, resourcefulness and hope (Flaskas, McCarthy and Sheehan 2007). It is therefore particularly relevant for work with women who are experiencing, or have recently experienced, abuse at the hands of an intimate partner. Wood and Roche (2001) and Roche and Wood (2005) have taken some of these concepts and embedded them in an approach to social work with abused women, counteracting the woman blaming which can sometimes accompany such work. The following chapter will explore how these techniques can be utilised in working with abused women, enabling them to move from abuse to long-term safety and survival.

Chapter 7

Narrative Social Work and Counselling Intervention for Intimate Partner Violence

Mapping the journey

This book has presented the voices of the women who participated in this research as they described in external, internal and reflexive narrative modes the stories of their journeys from abuse to lives beyond abuse. Their narratives were individual, but the patterns of their experiences contained a shared and common direction. While each woman's personal experience, and therefore her narrative of this experience, contained the personal idiosyncratic details that make her story uniquely hers, the commonality of resistance, meaning making and identity transition which emerged in the analysis of these narratives, enabled the mapping of the contours of their journeys from abuse to survival.

Stages on the journey to safety

Intervention which is guided by this social work and counselling approach will involve a number of steps, though not necessarily in a rigidly given order. For the sake of clarity in the presentation of the approach here, however, it will be presented as a series of stages, though it is best to understand these merely as 'signposts' or 'pointers' of the journey to safety. The details and the timing of the journey's direction will vary from woman to woman, reflecting the idiosyncratic nature of each local relationship and its particular influence on each woman's identity and meaning construction within and about that relationship. Forcing a woman to follow the journey that may have been successful for other women, without recognition of her unique agency and resistance to her particular abusive situation, will not only be unhelpful, but will add a further burden to the woman who has sought or been referred for support, advice and/or counselling. To assist in the elucidation of this approach, it will be presented below in a series of diagrammatic formats, with each 'map' acting as a 'stepping stone' across the terrain of the women's journeys.

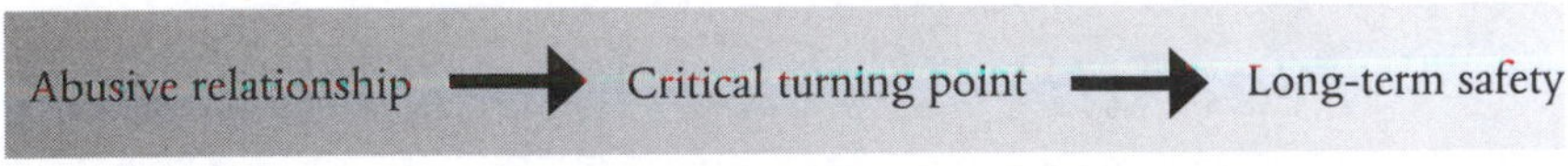

Figure 7.1 The journey's trajectory

Figure 7.1 represents the overall trajectory of the woman's journey away from an intimately abusive relationship to the ultimate destination of robust and long-term safety, which is the goal of this narrative approach. As discussed in detail in the Chapter 5, the turning point or catalyst for change on this journey may be an externally effective intervention or an internal reorientation in her resistance strategy – the realisation that 'enough is enough' and that the situation will not change.

The professional encounter

Figure 7.2 represents the first step in this overall journey, which is, as was seen in the participants' narratives, of variable length for each woman. Figure 7.2 represents the abused woman's initial interaction with the social work process. This interaction normally occurs after some critical turning point event or realisation, and may therefore be either voluntarily chosen by her or imposed on her by an external agency.

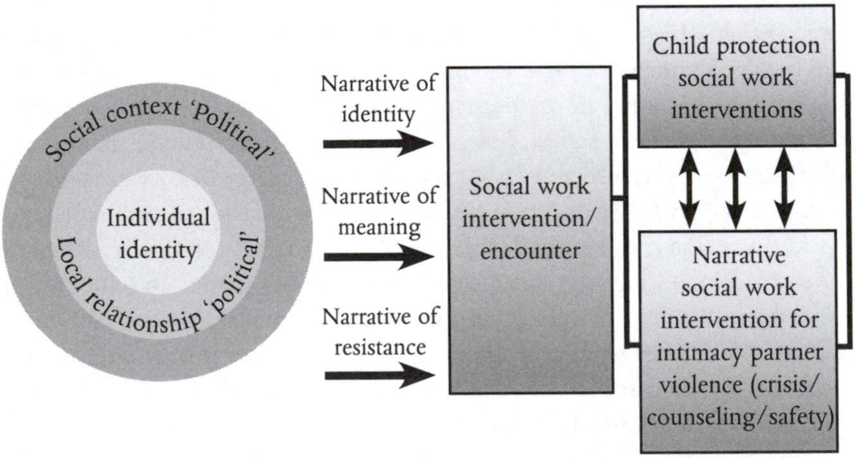

Figure 7.2 Social work encounter

The individual woman

On the left of the diagram is a representation of the individual woman, with her unique, flexible and socially constructed identity and personal historical and contemporary narrative. These personal and family narratives intersect with the cultural narratives and discourses which in turn shape both her identity and the meaning she constructs for her relationship and the abuse within it. She is located in the centre of a 'nested' local intimate relationship, with its particular local politics of control and abuse (politics in this case with a small 'p'), which is in turn located within the wider sociocultural 'Political' (with a capital 'P') societal system. She comes to the professional encounter therefore with her experiences of abuse, resistance, identity and meaning constructions. (This is represented by three arrows which connect her to the professional intervention context.) These arrows suggest that she brings not just the narrative of abuse, but a corresponding narrative of resistance, which includes, as was seen in the narratives of the participants in this book, and in the literature which was reviewed, the construction and reconstruction of the meaning of the relationship as she attempts to reduce the dissonance between the abuse and her understanding of her intimate relationship. This understanding of the individual woman 'nested' in her local relationship which is in turn nested in wider societal domains, illustrates the value of utilising both constructivist and social constructionist perspectives in the model of analysis which underpins this intervention approach.

Professional encounter

The central rectangle represents the social work or counselling encounter with this unique individual. As has been discussed previously, this encounter can be a highly contested activity. In response to the conflicts of interest between child protection concerns and the protection and support of women that can arise in practice, this model is proposing an alternative practice which can provide a 'structural solution' to this 'structural' problem.

Child protection pressures, as has been was discussed, jostle for time and attention with the woman's need for empowerment and support, and it would appear from the literature and research (Holt 2003; Humphreys 2000), that they almost always win this unequal contest. This literature would suggest that within the current mandates of statutory social work, one social worker cannot be 'all things' to both women and children. Consequently, two social workers working with a family would rebalance this inequality and ensure that the needs of both the woman and her children are heard and addressed. A similar model for example is used in the Guardiam ad Litem system (a guardian appointed by the court to protect the rights of the child) (Shannon 2003) where the need to balance and represent the needs of both children and their parents is acknowledged and legislated for. In the alternative practice proposed here, each worker, while taking a holistic approach to the needs of both mother and children, would focus their time and expertise on the needs of either the woman or children.

As Buckley, Whelan and Holt (2006) and Stanley and Humphreys (2006) point out, little therapeutic work is currently carried out with children who have witnessed or experienced domestic violence. Assigning a worker to work specifically with the children would serve to highlight the need for such work and provide the time and opportunity to do so. This worker, in the course of such work, would also be able to establish the safety needs of the children, and advocate for the necessary steps to be taken to ensure such safety. Counterbalancing this, the social worker assigned to the woman would ensure that the material and legal needs and options of the mother, as well as her need for support and empowerment, are appropriately addressed, not only in the short term but also in the later stages of her journey to safety.

Participative and ethical practices

In its efforts to contest the 'negative rhetoric and relationships of oppressive power' (McCarthy 2001, p.259) which can surface in social work and therapeutic contexts, the Fifth Province Model proposes a number of practices which would facilitate emancipatory and participative practice. Adapted for work specifically with situations of IPV, these practices would include:

- the development of participatory ethics wherein the woman's stories and issues are privileged
- juxtaposing and remembering dominant and local narratives on violence, intimate relationships and power
- involving a resource person from the client's community (this could be a friend or an advocate from a refuge or Women's Aid)
- linking the private issues of violence in this particular woman's relationship to the public issue of violence and gender orders.

The management of practice where there are two social workers working with the same family may at first glance present some difficulties in terms of decision making and information sharing. Different approaches may lead to conflicts between the social workers themselves. They may also present the woman with fears that only one worker is hearing her 'voice'. She may also find herself in the difficult position of having to 'mediate' between the differing approaches of the two practitioners. An awareness of these potential difficulties is necessary for the effective working out of this alternative 'dual' approach. Kennedy and O'Shaughnessy's (1998) practice of 'political conversations' between co-therapists provides an appropriate mechanism not only for overcoming these possible problems, but also for enhancing emancipatory practice. The two workers would meet at agreed intervals, together with the woman (preferably not less than once every two weeks), and if she wished, would also meet with her resource person (This could be a support worker from a refuge or a women's support group). They would talk to each other about their understandings of the situation and the specific interventions that might have been suggested. Equally important as the practical/legal issues, these conversations would also involve the workers linking this woman's experience of intimate partner violence with the wider cultural narratives and gender discourses which influence this violence. They would also link the structural barriers to her finding safety (e.g. economic dependence, experiences with the legal/housing systems) with these cultural narratives. They would invite the woman (if she wishes) to comment on these conversations, thereby providing another forum for her voice to be heard in the overall pattern of social work intervention. These 'political conversations', premised as they are on an awareness of the privileging of statutory power in social work encounters, provide a 'semi-public space' (Kennedy and O'Shaughnessy 1998, p.19) for previously unheard or even dismissed voices and perspectives, enabling genuinely collaborative practice to emerge. Regular supervision of this alternative practice approach would ensure genuinely effective as well as emancipatory practice by both practitioners.

This dual approach to balancing the needs of both women and their children is represented in Figure 7.2 by the division of the right-hand side rectangle into two separate but closely interrelated rectangles. The upper rectangle represents the intervention processes undertaken by the social worker working with the children, while the lower rectangle represents the intervention steps and counselling approaches with the woman on her own (which are set out in the final sections of this chapter). These interventions focus on the empowerment of the woman for her own protection and ultimately for the protection of her children. However, as this book does not explore the issues which are specifically relevant to child protection or child welfare, it will focus in more detail only on the interventions appropriate to the lower rectangle.

Challenges for practice

The adoption of this suggested approach may present a number of administrative difficulties in busy social work teams. First, suggesting that two social workers are needed to work with one family would place extra strains on already overstretched staff. In current circumstances this may severely challenge the ability of social work departments to be able to implement this suggested approach. However, the in-depth work with both women and children that this approach proposes, would increase women's safety and empower their decision-making process. Such outcomes would be likely to reduce the need for ongoing social work involvement in the longer term and in this way could result in the overall use of fewer rather than more resources.

A further and perhaps more serious challenge to the willingness of teams to consider this proposed approach may be the unintended but understandable perception of an implied criticism of current practice. Such perceptions would make social workers reluctant to adopt alternative procedures, particularly in view of the workload implications discussed above. Such perceptions could be allayed through the participation of practitioners by means of post-qualifying educational programmes. Such programmes would build on the considerable expertise of current practitioners, and by elucidating the theoretical and research underpinnings of the proposed model and approaches, could be seen as an enhancement rather than a critique of contemporary practice.

Working with identity, meaning and resistance

Safety and crisis resolution may, however, initially be the woman's major concern, particularly if this encounter is her first attempt to seek professional help. For the purposes of clarity, the intervention approach will be presented in three separate stages. Within these stages, the interrelationship of identity, meaning and resistance, will be highlighted and clarified.

Stage 1: Safety first (versus safety only)

Finding resistance

The narratives of the participants and the findings of other research reviewed all highlight the range of resistant responses in which women have engaged to protect both themselves and their children from increasing patterns of abuse, while at the same time (re)claiming their own identity within an increasingly incongruent context of meaning. The first point of contact, therefore, with a professional social worker or counsellor must recognise and honour these complex processes. Awareness of these processes must take equal precedence with an awareness of and concern for the physical safety of the woman and her children. Fears for a woman's safety tend to dominate early professional interventions, and this is entirely appropriate. It becomes inappropriate, however, when these concerns overwhelm and silence the voice of resistance and agency. To take a 'safety first' approach runs two risks: first, it risks silencing the narratives of resistance and agency, narratives which, as was seen in this book, dominate each woman's own story of abuse, and at the same time reveal her construction of meaning and the exercise of agency within the locally oppressive relationship; second, 'safety first' can easily become 'safety only', leading to further oppression of a woman who has developed a myriad of survival and resistance skills. By focusing only on immediate physical safety, practitioners may enforce their own layer of control, justifying it on either concerns about the woman's or (more likely) the children's physical safety. The first task of this enhanced social work/ counselling intervention, therefore, is to hold and acknowledge both these aspects of the woman's experience.

Narrating resistance

Taking cognisance of the risks to a woman's safety, particularly at the time of seeking external help or negotiating a change in the power dynamics of an abusive relationship, this intervention approach will begin with the voice and therefore the concerns of the abused woman. Appropriate and helpful questions at this point will be broad open questions, for example:

> 'Can you tell me what has been happening for you?'
>
> 'Can you tell me how you have been managing the situation up to now?'
>
> 'What have you been doing to keep yourself safe?'
>
> 'How has that worked for you?'
>
> 'What has changed recently?'
>
> 'What would you need to feel safer from now on?'

Questions such as these are examples of what can be described as 'open invitations to begin her narrative'. They help to create a space and dynamic in this particular professional relationship which will enable the abused woman to feel she can articulate her own voice. They are questions which enable the woman to narrate the 'external narrative' of her experience. They also reflect the 'not knowing' stance of collaborative therapy discussed in greater detail in Chapter 6. Within that voice there will be clear indications of the levels of danger and risk to both herself and her children, as well as the strategies of resistance and safety seeking at which she will be adept, but which she may not fully appreciate. It is necessary for the social worker or counsellor to bear in mind that most abused women will have spent years honing these resistance strategies, years when they may either have maintained a total silence about the abuse, or if it was known to her family or friends, years attempting to justify the relationship and perhaps even the partner's behaviour.

Recruiting an audience

As was described in Chapter 6, the technique of recruiting an audience (White 2007) of those who would have seen these resistances can help to surface and honour them at this point in the intervention. Questions which would be appropriate in recruiting this audience might be:

> 'Who saw you as stubborn (hard working/'mouthy') etc.?'
>
> 'Who saw you stand up for yourself?'
>
> 'Who saw you challenge him on that occasion?'
>
> 'What would they say to you about that?'
>
> 'How would that help you to respond to his abuse?'
>
> 'What would they say to you now about your relationship with him?'

As she may not have heard support and appreciation for these strategies from informal or formal external sources, this recruited 'audience' can help to validate her narratives of resistance. Such validation of her 'small acts of daily living', to borrow the term Wade (1997) borrowed from Goffman (1961), focuses the conversation on the next steps to safety and survival.

Barriers to finding resistance

At this point of the intervention, questions which focus narrowly on children's safety, ignoring their mother's ingenuity and courage in protecting them from violence, will counteract the effectiveness of this 'open invitation' and influence a narrow and defensive narrative – echoing the dominant discourses of the responsibilities of motherhood which have led to the 'mixed' outcomes of social work with abused women in child protection settings. Women are rarely if ever unaware of the risks to their children from abusive partners. Recognition of their efforts to counteract these risks, as was demonstrated by many of the participants in this book, will strengthen the invitation to share their stories of resistance to the abuse. These stories can also inform and enhance the interventions being undertaken by the children's social worker, in situations where the allocation of a separate worker has been thought appropriate.

Other resources

Intervention at this early stage may also involve referral to a Women's Refuge or other place of safety, either on a temporary or semi-permanent basis. It will probably involve advice regarding the legal options open to a woman, such as a safety or a barring order. It may involve referral to a legal aid solicitor, or to the court accompaniment service of a specialised domestic violence service.

Stage 2: Going further (and deeper)

Finding meaning and identity

Once the immediate danger to the woman (and/or her children) has been assessed and appropriate strategies to increase her safety have been negotiated and implemented by her and with her, the next stage of this intervention model can be given greater emphasis. (It is important to keep in mind that safety is not a 'once off' achievement. The woman and the social worker/counsellor may need to return to the issues of safety, legal processes and accommodation a number of times.)

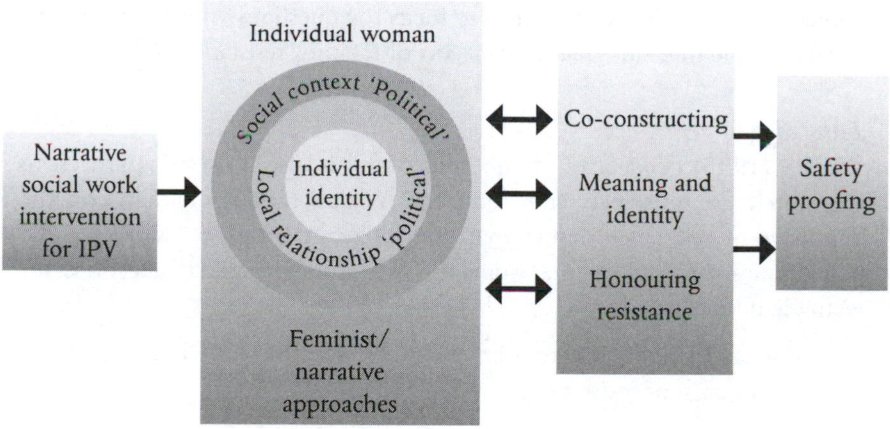

Figure 7.3 Creating a feminist therapeutic space

Figure 7.3 demonstrates both the shape and consequences of the therapeutic space where the woman can take the time to reflect on her experiences within the safety of a non-judgemental and supportive professional relationship. The counselling task within this space is represented by the two larger central rectangles. To create this therapeutic space, however, the professional must be aware of, and be able to assist her to surface the elements which are central to this understanding of her experiences. The focus of the social worker or counsellor, therefore, at this stage of the intervention process is to search for and honour resistance, identity and meaning construction in the woman's narrative.

Narrative approaches

As has been discussed earlier, narrative counselling techniques are particularly appropriate to this task, grounded in a constructivist epistemology with a sensitivity to a feminist analysis of the power of patriarchal domination. Allied to this is the poststructuralist influence of Foucault's (1980) understanding of the techniques of power, and the insurrection of local knowledges, concepts which are central to an appreciation of resistance within a local intimate relationship.

These distinctive narrative techniques, allied to the repertoire of a social worker's or counsellor's listening and empathic relationship building skills, are appropriate tools in this intervention model. The Narrative Process Theory (Angus *et al.* 1999) for example, which, as discussed in Chapter 6, divides the storying of experience into external, internal and reflective modes, is an appropriate structure around which to focus the questions which facilitate the naming of the three interrelated concepts of identity, resistance and meaning.

Language of resistance

White's (1995) concept of 'unique outcomes' is also a useful approach to the search for resistance, and Todd and Wade's (2003) emphasis on the 'language of resistance' rather than the language of effects will keep the conversation focused on the woman's own strategies. Such questions for example might include:

> 'What did you say to him when he wanted you to do that?' (Language of resistance.)
>
> 'Had you ever argued with him about that issue before?' (Language of resistance.)
>
> 'What were you thinking when you decided to go along with him for "peace sake"?' (Language of resistance.)

'Describe what changed when you didn't do what he wanted you to do?' (Unique outcome question.)

'What else did you do that made life easier for you?' (Unique outcome question.)

Keeping a journal may also help a woman to focus on the power of her own strategies, affirming and strengthening her small (and sometimes large) insurrections.

Finding meaning and identity

An essential element of this stage of the intervention process is the recognition and naming of the social construction of the discourses of gender and the systematic incorporation of these discourses into the wider sociocultural system in which the individual woman, her family of origin, her partner, and their relationship are located. Enabling the woman to reflect on these discourses, and the extent to which they were formative and/or facilitative of the abuse of power by her partner, is necessary to enable her to place the meaning of her relationship, and the meaning of abuse within that relationship, within the wider societal construction of romance and familial discourses.

Narrating meaning and identity

Questions influenced by the Narrative Process Theory (Angus *et al.* 1999) can help to find and narrate these meanings. External narrative questions enable the opening up of the intervention process. Internal and reflexive narrative questions can now enable the exploration of meaning:

'What were your hopes for the relationship when you married (moved in) with your partner/husband?' (Internal narrative.)

'How did you imagine it would work out?' (Internal narrative.)

'What did your family/friends think about your relationship?' (Reflexive narrative.)

'What did you begin to think when the abuse/control began?' (Internal narrative.)

'How did your partner/husband explain his behaviour?' (Internal narrative.)

'Did that make sense to you?' (Reflexive narrative.)

'Where do you think he got those ideas?' (Reflexive narrative.)

> 'Who else in your community/family held those kinds of ideas?' (Reflexive narrative).
>
> 'Where do you think they came from?' (Reflexive narrative).

This narrative process will also enable her to recognise the manner in which she resisted these discourses at the local level – and in doing so, how she resisted the imposition of the unwanted identity of the 'battered woman'. Questions which may help with this narrating of her identity would be:

> 'How would you describe the (young) woman who began this relationship?'
>
> 'How did you see yourself when the abuse began?'
>
> 'How did you see yourself as you did (example of resistance) to protect yourself?'
>
> 'How do you see yourself now that the relationship is ending/over?'
>
> 'Can you describe the woman who has got to this point?'

All of these processes will clearly not occur in one session, and, as discussed above, may be interspersed with the practicalities of legal, housing or safety concerns. While these counselling and practical issues may be separated conceptually, they are of course not separate in reality. They are all part of the journey to safety, but, as with any complicated and challenging journey where the precise destination is not known, there will need to be constant checking and rechecking of the goals of the journey, the possible choice of roads that can be taken, the areas that are best bypassed and the ones that need to be visited. For this reason, the map may need to be redrawn on a regular basis, depending on the exigencies of external circumstances (e.g. children's schooling needs, economic necessity, illness, increased partner violence, insufficient police support). Within this uncertainty of destination and navigation, however, the counselling process will continue to elucidate and foreground the woman's preferred identity, her meaning construction of the relationship, the meaning of intimacy, the meaning of abuse and control, and the relationship of her strategies of resistance (small as they may seem to her) to these constructions of meaning and evolving identity. This process leads to the co-construction of the woman's new meanings and preferred identity, and is represented by the two way arrows connecting the central two rectangles in Figure 7.3.

Stage 3: Nearing the destination

Figure 7.4 summarises women's overall journey from abuse to safety. However, this book seeks to emphasise, in a way which has not been sufficiently emphasised previously, the later, post-separation stage of the journey. This stage involves safety proofing and 'robust long-term safety', both of which contribute to the concept of 'survival resistance'.

Figure 7.4 A journey to safety

Safety proofing

The third stage of this intervention approach can be described as 'safety-proofing' for the woman's future, and is represented by the rectangle on the right of Figure 7.3. It is sometimes assumed that once a woman takes a legal order (e.g. a protection or a barring order) or moves to a refuge, that the social worker's or support person's job is done. She (and her children) are now safe. This is the risk of 'safety first' becoming 'safety only'. What others may see as the ultimate success of their interventions, is, for the woman, just the first step on a long, difficult and life-changing journey. If she is left without ongoing support at this point of making life-changing decisions, she may find that she is unable to take herself to an unknown destination without a road map and or apparent means of getting there. One of the consequences of this challenge may be the choice or need for the woman to return to her partner, either temporarily or permanently. The third step of the *Narrative Intervention for Intimate Partner Violence* is therefore as important as the previous stages. As mentioned previously, there has been little emphasis in the social work or counselling literature to date on this stage of the leaving process. It is at this point that long-term decisions will need to be made. A range of narrative style questions which will be helpful at this stage, and which foreground her preferred identity, are:

> 'How would you describe yourself at this point?' (Identity question.)
>
> 'Is this the woman you wanted to be when you got married?' (Preferred identity question.)
>
> 'Who do you want to be in the future?' (Preferred identity question.)
>
> 'What are you doing to become this woman?' (Action question).
>
> 'Who can help you in this?' (Resourcing question).

'What would they say to (or do for) you now?' (Witness question.)

'If you take this step, what will they say about you?' (Witness question.)

'Who will you be if you do this?' (Preferred identity question.)

Reconstruction of identity

Decisions taken at this point may involve leaving her partner permanently or temporarily. They may involve accepting and acknowledging the permanent loss of the relationship to which she had optimistically committed herself, and which she strategically and courageously worked to maintain for many years. The social worker will therefore need to be acutely aware of the woman's grief for such loss. The loss will not only be for her relationship, but will also involve a loss of identity as partner or wife, and of the dream of having a 'normal, happy' family life. It will involve the recognition and acceptance of a new 'evolving' identity to which it will take time (and pain) to adapt. The narrative of her journey to her new identity will itself be constitutive of that identity and it will take time and skill by the social worker or counsellor to facilitate this transformative narrative.

Survival resistance

As with her experience of surviving an abusive relationship, her post-separation experiences will also involve what has been identified as 'survival resistance'. This may involve legal battles for access to and custody of children, or the transfer and ownership of property. It may involve, as the analysis of the narratives in this book suggested, resisting ongoing harassment and threats. It may involve getting a new job, taking up educational opportunities, becoming a single parent to possibly angry and traumatised children, or moving to a new neighbourhood. It will require ongoing reconstruction of the meaning of these experiences, similar to those who are bereaved, but with the added grief of disappointment, regret and possibly ongoing fear. Narrative techniques, such as transition ceremonies, diaries and journals (which were outlined in Chapter 6) may be helpful in marking and, where possible, celebrating the stages of the journey which have been reached, and their meaning in the overall goal of co-constructing her preferred future with a preferred, now clearly evolving identity. This identity will be informed by both a woman's previous identity and by her experiences of surviving, and increasingly, thriving.

Narrating survival resistance, identity and meaning

The *Narrative Intervention for Intimate Partner Violence* will continue to be informed and guided by the integration of the three concepts of identity, meaning and resistance, which were identified by and are central to this approach. Questions which would be helpful in guiding this 'survival' stage of the intervention process would be for example:

> 'How would you describe yourself now?' (Identity question.)
>
> 'What have you done to become this woman?' (Action question.)
>
> 'How did you know you had the strength to do all this?' (Resistance question.)
>
> 'How did you overcome the stories of your family/partner/culture?' (Resistance question.)
>
> 'How would you now understand an intimate relationship?' (Meaning question.)
>
> 'What would you now say about your husband/partner's views on men and women?' (Meaning question.)
>
> 'What would you like to do to liberate other women who are being abused/oppressed/controlled?' (Resistance question.)

As a result of the 'safety proofing' which results from the counselling and safety interventions integral to this new intervention approach, the woman at this point of the process will herself now know what her future needs for support may be and how she will fulfil them. The social worker or counsellor will take her or his lead from the woman's own assessment, leaving possibilities for future contact open if the need should arise. The woman's journey is not of course concluded – all human journeys continue as our identities evolve with our individual experiences, and as our narratives of those experiences shape our identities. The journey from abuse to survival is, however, almost completed. It is unlikely that it is ever fully over for severely abused women, as they carry the memory and the pain of that journey into the next stages and future experiences of their lives.

Having travelled from the optimism of the beginnings of a romantic relationship, through the terrain of abuse, resistance, change, safety and survival, it can be suggested that a woman now returns home to herself and her dreams for the future.

Concluding summary

This book set out to enable the contemporary discourses informing the issue of intimate partner violence to be integrated into practice with abused women. It has drawn on both historical and contemporary material and on previously published and original research. Building on this information and experience, it has presented a theoretical model of women's journeys from abusive relationships, through critical turning point(s), to long-term safety. This model has highlighted, in a manner which has not been highlighted or elucidated previously, the concepts *of narrative identity*, *meaning construction*, and *ongoing strategies of resistance* in the processes of women's decision making and safety seeking. Safety has been seen to include *safety first*, *safety proofing* and post-separation *survival resistance*. The book has utilised this analytical model to scaffold an enhanced approach to social work and counselling interventions with abused women which it has titled *Narrative Intervention for Intimate Partner Violence*. This practice approach has been grounded primarily in the analysis of the participants' narratives, but also in wider research and literature in the fields of both domestic violence and contemporary therapeutic approaches. The model has used the analogy of a map in navigating a hazardous journey, an analogy which recognises that leaving an abusive relationship is a complex and lengthy process rather than a clear-cut once off decision or event. In tracing this journey and facilitating its appropriate arrival at safety, the role of narrative and language has been emphasised. It seems appropriate therefore to end with the reflective words of one of the participants, without whose voices and 'survival resistance' this book and model of practice could not have been possible.

> **Rose:** Its always the first question – what did you stay for? I suppose I am looking at it from two different perspectives now. I'm looking at it like people that don't understand it, to say that she's a victim, and they're going to feel sorry for her. Not seeing her as a strong individual to stay in this relationship, to try to make it work, for her kids, for her family. To try to keep the family unit together. They're not seeing her as this strong person that she really is – they're seeing her as weak. That's what we don't want – to be seen as weak.

Appendix

Feminist standpoint epistemology

Maynard (1994, p.14) summarises the feminist research task succinctly: 'Feminism must begin with experience, it has been argued, since it is only from such a vantage point that it is possible to see the extent to which women's worlds are organised in ways which differ from those of men.' In response to this need to see the world from women's vantage points, feminist standpoint epistemology (also known as 'women's experience epistemology') suggested an alternative approach to research methodology (Letherby 2003, p.44). In contrast to the detached and analytically oriented approach to science and the production of objective knowledge, standpoint epistemology, it was believed 'would lead to a holistic, integrated, connected knowledge' (Millen 1997, p.7.2). Haraway (1997, p.304), one of the leading contributors to standpoint research theory, defines standpoints as 'cognitive – emotional – political achievements, crafted out of located social–historical–bodily experience – itself always constituted through fraught, non-innocent, discursive, material collective practices.' From this starting point, Harding suggests that the experience and lives of marginalised people, as they understand them, provide the most significant agendas for the feminist research process (1993).

Despite its influence on feminist research and theory, standpoint epistemology is not without its critics. As Letherby (2003) notes, the suggestion that one group's perspective is more valid or more real than another's, is questionable. It is possible that a feminist standpoint can replace male supremacy with female supremacy! Standpoint approaches may also fall victim to the charge of 'essentialism' (Lemert 1992, p.69) which tends to limit the experiences of women to those which resonate with traditional identities, for example, that of victim. Gender is experienced in diverse ways by diverse groups of women, and women exercise varying levels of power in varying circumstances, which Hartsock (1990, p.171) describes as the 'concrete multiplicity' of perspectives. The debates which have raised and answered these claims (Olesen 2000) make it clear that not only is standpoint epistemology not a single approach, it is constantly being revised, incorporating theoretical developments from the various disciplines which contributed to its development. For example, Harding (1996) specifically refers to poststructural contributions which enable standpoint theories to critique the exercise of power as shaped not just by gender, but by class, race and other cultural forces, which are in turn disseminated through structural and symbolic discourses.

Postmodern / poststructural feminist theories

As well as their profound influence on every aspect of contemporary human sciences, postmodern and poststructural theories have also made important contributions to feminist theory. Harding understands these latter theories as contributing to a 'voiding' of the possibility of a feminist science, to be replaced by the multiple stories women tell about the knowledge they have (Olesen 2000, p.223). From the perspective of postmodernism, there cannot be one universal truth. Truth is rather located only in the values and interests of particular groups. Consequently, any attempt to establish a universal truth or theory is oppressive or an illusion (Letherby 2003). From this perspective searching for a unitary truth about the world is impossible, because knowledge is partial, profane and fragmented (McLennan 1995). Millen (1997, p.7) suggests that rather than seeking out a unifying epistemology, even one which incorporates gender, 'we should be constructing multiple discourses.' Such a postmodernist approach has been criticised as 'relativist', and in its strictest interpretation, makes an impossibility of theory building for practice in any unified sense.

Despite the 'cultural turn' within academic feminism, it is not, according to Maynard (1994, p.20) necessary to entirely jettison structuralist contributions to our understanding of women's experiences: 'It is after all possible to acknowledge the significance of culture and discourse and some of the problems to which they may give rise in speaking about the social world, without denying that events, relations and structures do have conditions of existence and real effects outside the sphere of the discursive.' Such an inclusive approach to theorising is echoed by Olesen (2000) who suggests that feminist research projects draw on elements of several available epistemological approaches. Kelly, Burton and Regan (1994, p.46) are quite adamant when they comment that 'most of the methods which have been endorsed as "feminist" were not created by feminism: in-depth interviews, ethnography, grounded theory and action research all have non-feminist origins and histories.' Reinharz suggests (1992) that feminism supplies the perspective, while individual disciplines supply the methods.

It must therefore be concluded that there is no one single research method that can claim to be *the* feminist method. However, standpoint theories and postmodern influences can provide a 'gender lens' to guide the choice of methodology in a study which explores women's experiences of, and responses to, intimate partner violence. Such a methodology should be able to take account of the sensitivity of the issues involved, while remaining open to the possibility of diversity amongst the narratives of these experiences.

The following criteria have been identified as necessary in research undertaken about and with women from a feminist standpoint approach:

- Feminist research tries to take women's needs, interests and experiences into account and aims at being instrumental in improving women's lives in one way or another (Duelli-Klein 1983, p.90).
- It should provide understandings of women's experiences as they understand it, interpreted in the light of feminist conceptions of gender relations (Ramazanoglu 1989).
- Feminist research methods are methods used in research projects by people who identify themselves as feminist or as part of the women's movement (Reinharz 1992, p.6).
- Feminist research uses both women's own 'different' experience as its point of departure and processes this experience in a manner which leads to liberating knowledge (Lundgren 1995, p.25).
- It values the private and personal as worthy of study (Letherby 2003, p.73).
- It develops non-exploitative relationships within research (Letherby 2003, p.73).
- It values reflexivity and emotion as a source of insight as well as an essential part of research (Letherby 2003, p.73).

Constructivist grounded theory

Qualitative methods are generally viewed as being sensitive to women's experiences as seen from their perspectives, and as empowering in the transformative challenge to research (Henwood and Pidgeon 1992). The methodological approach chosen to fulfil the needs of this research project as outlined above is constructivist grounded theory. As the title suggests, this is a more recent development (Charmaz 2000, 2003, 2005) of the well known and popular methodology originally developed by Glaser and Strauss (1967, 1978) and later by Strauss and Corbin (1990, 1998). At its simplest, grounded theory can be described as a general methodology for developing theory that is grounded in data which are gathered and analysed in a systematic fashion (Strauss and Corbin 1998). As originally presented by Glaser and Strauss (1967) in *The Discovery of Grounded Theory*, the theory was a counterpoint to the then dominant structural functionalism of contemporary sociology (as represented particularly by Parsons 1968 and Merton 1945) which they regarded as overly deductive and speculative (Strauss and Corbin 1998; Charmaz 2000, 2003). This methodology moved social science research away from the hypothetico-deductive method of theory development to an 'inductive' approach in which the meanings which individuals constructed for things and relationships in their environment could be formulated in an emergent manner (Whiteley 2004, p.31). In this way, theory is generated from data, or may elaborate and modify existing (grounded) theories if they seem appropriate to an area of investigation (Strauss and Corbin 1998).

Charmaz's constructivist grounded theory, on the other hand, claims to use grounded theory's guidelines as tools for analysis while not subscribing to the 'objectivist, positivist assumptions' she critiqued in Glaser, Strauss and Corbin's works (Charmaz 2005, p.509). Charmaz's development of the theory takes a 'middle ground' between positivism and postmodernism, as it 'assumes the relativism of multiple social realities, recognises the mutual creation of knowledge by the viewer and the viewed, and aims towards interpretive understanding of subject's meanings' (Charmaz 2003, p.250).

The concept of 'purposive' or 'theoretical' sampling (Strauss and Corbin 1998, p.201) guided the determination of the size of the sample, and the researcher continued to approach agencies until it was felt that no new material or concepts were emerging from the interview analysis. The concept of 'theoretical sampling' according to Chamaz (2003, p.265) represents a defining property of grounded theory. The aim of theoretical sampling is to refine ideas, and to test the fit and relevance of the categories and themes. Returning to the participants for a second interview facilitated theoretical sampling by permitting the researcher to explore the tentative theoretical framework which appeared to be emerging from the simultaneous conceptual analysis. The second interview also facilitated the collaborative methodology which maximised the participants' voice and representation in the research.

References

Abels, P. and Abels, S.L. (2001) *Understanding Narrative Therapy. A Guidebook for the Social Worker.* New York: Springer Publishing Company.

Allen, M. (2011) 'Violence and voice: Using a feminist constructivist grounded theory to explore women's resistance to abuse.' *Qualitative Research 11*, 1, 23–45.

Allen, M. and Perttu, S. (2010) *Teachers' Handbook. HEVI* – Social and Health Care Teachers Against Violence. Available at www.palmenia.helsinki.fi/hevi/HEVI_Handbook_english.pdf, accessed 20 July 2011.

Anderson, H. (1997) *Language and Possibilities: A Postmodern Approach to Therapy.* New York: Basic Books.

Anderson, H. (2007) 'The heart and spirit of collaborative therapy: The philosophical stance – "a way of being" in relationship conversation.' In H. Anderson and D. Gerhart (eds) *Collaborative Therapy: Relationships and Conversations that Make a Difference.* New York: Routledge.

Anderson, D.K. and Saunders, D.G. (2003) 'Leaving an abusive partner: An empirical review of predictors, the process of leaving, and psychological well-being.' *Trauma, Violence and Abuse 4*, 2, 163–190.

Angell, R.C. (1936) *The Family Encounters the Depression.* New York: Charles Scribner.

Angus, L., Levitt, H. and Hardtke, K. (1999) 'The Narrative Processes Coding System: Research applications and implications for psychotherapy practice.' *Journal of Clinical Psychology 55*, 10, 1255–1270.

Archer, J. (2000) 'Sex difference in aggression between heterosexual partners: A meta-analytical review.' *Psychology Bulletin 126*, 5, 651–680.

Baker, P.L. (1997) 'And I went back: Battered women's negotiation of choice.' *Journal of Contemporary Ethnography 26*, 55–74.

Bandura, A. (1973) *Aggression: A Learning Analysis.* Upper Saddle River, NJ: Prentice Hall.

Bateson, G. (1972) *Steps to an Ecology of Mind: Collected Essays in Anthropology, Psychiatry, Evolution and Epistemology.* New York: Chandler.

Bateson, G. (1979) *Mind and Nature: A Necessary Unity.* New York: Dutton.

Berger, P. and Luckmann, T. (1967) *The Social Construction of Reality.* Garden City, NY: Anchor Books.

Birns, B. *et al.* (1994) 'Sex-role socialization: Developmental influences on wife abuse.' *American Orthopsychiatric Association 64*, 1.

Black, D.A., Schumacher, J.A., Smith, S. and Heyman, R.E. (1999) *Partner, Child Abuse Risk Factors: Literature Review.* National Network of Family Resiliency, National Network for Health (www.nnh.org/risk).

Brown, C. (2007) 'Situating knowledge and power in the therapeutic alliance.' In C. Brown and T. Augusta-Scott (eds) *Narrative Therapy. Making Meaning, Making Lives.* Thousand Oaks, CA: Sage.

Brown, C. and Augusta-Scott, T. (eds) (2007) *Narrative Therapy. Making Meaning, Making Lives.* Thousand Oaks, CA: Sage.

Bruner, J. (1986) *Actual Minds, Possible Worlds.* Cambridge, MA: Harvard University Press.

Bruner, J. (1990) *Acts of Meaning.* Cambridge, MA: Harvard University Press.

Buckley, H., Whelan, S. and Holt, S. (2006) *Listen to Me: Children's Experience of Domestic Violence.* Dublin: TCD Children's Research Centre.

Burke, P.J. and Stets, J.E. (2009) *Identity Theory.* New York: Oxford University Press.

Campbell, J., Rose, L., Kub, J. and Nedd, D. (1998) 'Voices of strength and resistance: A contextual and longitudinal analysis of women's responses to battering.' *Journal of Interpersonal Violence 13,* 6, 743–762.

Carr, A. (2002) 'Narrative therapy: One perspective on the work of Michael White.' *Feedback 9.*

Cavan, B. and Ranck, K.H. (1938) *Family and the Depression: A Study of One Hundred Chicago Families.* Chicago, IL: University of Chicago Press.

Cavanagh, K., Dobash, R.E., Dobash, R.P. and Lewis, R. (2001) '"Remedial work": Men's strategic responses to their violence against intimate female partners.' *Sociology 35,* 3, 695–714.

Centre for Disease Control and Surveillance (2008) *Behavioural Risk Factor Surveillance Survey 2005.* Available at www.cdc.gov/brfss/technical_infodata/surveydata/2005.htm, accessed 8 September 2011.

Chang, J.C., Dado, D., Ashton, S., Hawker, L. *et al.* (2006) 'Understanding behavior change for women experiencing intimate partner violence: Mapping the ups and downs using the stages of change.' *Patient Education and Counseling 62,* 330–339.

Charmaz, K. (2000) 'Constructivist and objectivist grounded theory.' In N.R. Denzin and Y.S. Lincoln (eds) *Strategies of Qualitative Inquiry.* Thousand Oaks, CA: Sage, 509-535.

Charmaz, K. (2003) 'Grounded theory. Objectivist and constructivist methods.' In N.R. Denzin and Y.S. Lincoln (eds) *Strategies of Qualitative Inquiry.* Thousand Oaks, CA: Sage, pp.249–291.

Charmaz, K. (2005) 'Grounded theory in the 21st century. Applications for advancing social justice studies.' In N.R. Denzin and Y.S. Lincoln (eds) *Handbook of Qualitative Research.* Thousand Oaks, CA: Sage, pp.507–535.

Coates, L. and Wade, A. (2004) 'Telling it like it isn't: Obscuring perpetrator responsibility for violent crime.' *Discourse and Society 15,* 5, 499–526.

Cobbe, F.P. (1878) 'Wife torture in England.' In *The Contemporary Review* April, 55–87.

Coker, A.L.L., Watkins, K.W., Smith, P.H. and Brandt, H.M. (2003) 'Social support reduces the impact of partner violence on health: Application of structural equation models.' *Preventive Medicine 37,* 3, 259–267.

Coleman, K., Hird, C. and Povey, D. (2006) *Violent Crime Overview, Homicide and Gun Crime 2004/2005.* Home Office Statistical Bulletin 02/06. London: Home Office.

Council of Europe (2002) Recommendation Rec (2002): 5 of the Committee of Ministers to member States on the protection of women against violence adopted on 30 April 2002. Available at www.coe.int/t/e/human_rights/equality/05._violence_against_women

Currie, D.H. (1998) 'Violent men or violent women? Whose definition counts?' In R.K. Bergen (ed.) *Issues in Intimate Violence.* London: Sage.

Dobash, R.E. and Dobash, R. (1979) *Violence Against Wives: A Case Against the Patriarchy.* New York: The Free Press.

Dobash, R.E. and Dobash, R. (1992) *Women, Violence and Social Change.* London: Routledge.

Dobash, R.E. and Dobash, R.P. (eds) (1998) *Rethinking Violence Against Women.* Thousand Oaks, CA: Sage.

Dobash, R.P. and Dobash, R.E. (2004) 'Women's violence to men in intimate relationships.' *British Journal of Criminology 44,* 3, 324–349.

Dobash, R.E., Dobash, R.P., Cavanagh, K. and Medina-Ariza, J. (2007) 'Lethal and nonlethal violence against an intimate female partner: Comparing male murderers to nonlethal abusers.' *Violence Against Women 13,* 4, 329–353.

Dominelli, L. (2004) *Social Work: Theory and Practice for a Changing Profession.* Cambridge: Polity.

Duelli-Klein, R. (1983) 'How to do what we want to do?: Thoughts about feminist methodology.' In G. Bowles and R. Duelli-Klein (eds) *Theories of Women's Studies.* London: Routledge and Kegan Paul.

Dutton, M.A. (1996) 'The battered woman's strategic response to violence: The role of context.' In J.L. Edleson and Z.C. Eisikovits (eds) *Future Interventions with Battered Women and their Families.* London: Sage.

Eliot, T.S. (1943) *The Four Quartets.* London: Faber and Faber.

Ellesberg, M.C., Pena, R., Herrerra, A., Liljestrand, J. and Winkvist, A. (1999) 'Wife abuse among women of childbearing age in Nicaragua.' *American Journal of Public Health 89*, 2, p.241–244.

Erikson, E. (1959) *Identity and the Life Cycle.* New York: International University Press.

EU (2009) International Women's Day – The Commission's campaign to stop violence against women. Available at www.europa.eu

Fals-Stewart, W. (2003) 'The occurrence of partner physical aggression on days of alcohol consumption: A longitudinal diary study.' *Journal of Consulting and Clinical Psychology 71*, 1, 41–52.

Ferraro, K. and Johnson, J. (1983) 'How women experience battering: The process of victimization.' *Social Problems 30*, 3, 325–339.

Fiebert, M. (1997) 'Annotated bibliography: References examining assaults by women on their spouses/partners.' *Sexuality and Culture 1*, 273–286.

Flaskas, C., McCarthy, I. and Sheehan, J. (2007) *Hope and Despair in Narrative and Family Therapy.* Hove: Routledge.

Fook, J. (2002) *Social Work. Critical Theory and Practice.* London: Sage.

Forgey, M.A. and Badger, L. (2006) 'Patterns of intimate partner violence among married women in the military: Type, level, directionality and consequences.' *Journal of Family Violence 21*, 6, 369–380.

Foucault, M. (1980) *Power/Knowledge: Selected Interviews and Other Writings.* C. Gordon (ed.) New York: Pantheon.

Foucault, M. (1981) *The History of Sexuality. Volume 1.* Harmondsworth: Pelican.

Foucault, M. (1989) *Foucault Live: Interviews, 1966–1984.* New York: Semiotext.

Foucault, M. (1995) *Discipline and Punish: The Birth of the Prison* 2nd edn. New York: Vintage Books.

Frankl, V.E. (1962) *Man's Search for Meaning: An Introduction to Logotherapy.* Boston, MA: Beacon Press.

Fraser, N. and Nicholson, L. (1990) 'Social criticism without philosophy.' In L. Nicholson (ed.) *Feminism/Postmodernism.* London: Routledge.

Garcia-Moreno, C., Jansen, H.A.F.M., Ellsberg, M., Heise, L. and Watts, C.H. (2006) 'Prevalence of intimate partner violence: Findings from the WHO multi-country study on women's health and domestic violence.' *Lancet 368*, 9543, 1260–1269.

Gelles, R.J. (1974) *The Violent Home: A Study of Physical Aggression Between Husbands and Wives.* Beverly Hills, CA: Sage.

Gelles, R.J. and Straus, M.A. (1988) *Intimate Violence.* New York: Simon and Schuster.

Gergen, K. (1991) *The Saturated Self: Dilemma of Identity in Contemporary Life.* New York: Basic Books.

Giddens, A. (1991) *Modernity and Self-Identity: Self and Society in the Late Modern Age.* Cambridge: Polity Press.

Glaser, B.G. and Srauss, A.L. (1967) *The Discovery of Grounded Theory: Strategies for Qualitative Research*, Chicago, IL: Aldine

Glaser, B.G. and Strauss, A.L. (1978) *Grounded Theory: Sociological Methods*, New York: McGraw-Hill

Goffman, E. (1961) *Asylums: Essays in the Social Situation of Mental Patients and Other Inmates.* New York: Doubleday.

Goffman, E. (1974) *Frame Analysis: An Essay on the Organization of Experience.* London: Harper and Row.

Gondolf, E. and Fisher, E. (1988) *Battered Women as Survivors: An Alternative to Treating Learned Helplessness.* New York: Lexington Books.

Goodkind, J.R., Tameka, L.G., Bybee, D.I. and Sullivan, C.M. (2003) 'The impact of family and friends. Reactions on the well-being of women with abusive partners.' *Violence Against Women 9*, 3, 347–372.

Goodman, L., Dutton, M.A., Weinfurt, K. and Cook, S. (2003) 'The intimate partner violence strategies index.' *Violence Against Women 9*, 2, 163–186.

Goodman, L., Dutton, M.A., Vankos, N. and Weinfurt, K. (2005) 'Women's resources and use of strategies as risk and protective factors for reabuse over time.' *Violence Against Women 11*, 3, 311–336.

Graham-Kevan, N. and Archer, J. (2003) 'Intimate terrorism and common couple violence: A test of Johnson's predictions in four British samples.' *Journal of Interpersonal Violence 18*, 11, 1247–1270.

Graham, K., Bernards, S., Wilsnack, S.C. and Gmel, G. (2011) 'Alcohol may not cause partner violence, but it seems to make it worse: A cross national comparison of the relationship between alcohol and severity of partner abuse.' *Journal of Interpersonal Violence 26*, 8, 1503–1523.

Grant, A. (1999) 'Resistance to the link at a domestic violence shelter.' In F.R. Ascione and P. Arkow (eds) *Child Abuse, Domestic Violence and Animal Abuse.* West Lafayette, IN: Purdue University Press.

Gray, N. (2007) 'Responding to men's violence.' In A. Yuen and C. White (eds) *Conversations about Gender, Culture, Violence and Narrative Practice.* Adelaide: Dulwich Centre Publications.

Haj-Yahia, M.M. (2003) 'Beliefs about wife beating among Arab men from Israel: The influence of their patriarchal ideology.' *Journal of Family Violence 18*, 4, 193–206.

Hamberger, L.K. (2005) 'Men's and women's use of intimate partner violence in clinical samples: Toward a gender sensitive analysis.' *Violence Against Women 20*, 1, 131–152.

Hammons, A. (2004) '"Family violence": The language of legitimacy.' *Affilia 19*, 3, 273–288.

Hanmer, J. (2000) 'Domestic violence and gender relations; contexts and connections.' In J. Hanmer and C. Itzin (eds) *Home Truths About Domestic Violence.* London: Routledge.

Haraway, D.J. (1997) *Modest_Witness@second_ millennium:Femalman meets Oncomouse*, New York: Routledge.

Harding, S. (1993) 'Rethinking standpoint epistemology: "What is strong objectivity?"' In L. Alcoff and E. Potter (eds) *Feminist Epistemologies.* New York: Routledge.

Harding, S. (1996) 'Gendered ways of knowing and the "epistemological crisis" of the West.' In N. Goldberger, J. Tarule, B. Clinchy and M. Belenky (eds) *Knowledge, Difference and Power: Essays Inspired by Women's Ways of Knowing.* New York: Basic Books.

Hartsock, N. (1990) 'Foucault on power: A theory for women?' In L. Nicholson (ed.) *Feminism/ Postmodernism.* London: Routledge.

Hearn, J. (1998) *The Violences of Men: How Men Talk About and How Agencies Respond to Men's Violence to Women.* London: Sage.

Heise, L. (1998) 'Violence against women: An integrated, ecological framework.' *Violence Against Women 4*, 3, 262–290.

Heise, L. and Garcia-Moreno, C. (2002) 'Violence by intimate partners.' In E. Krug, L. Dahlberg, J.A. Mercy, A.B. Zwi and R. Lozano (eds) *World Report on Violence and Health.* Geneva: WHO.

Henwood, K.L. and Pidgeon, N.F. (1992) 'Qualitative research and psychological theorizing.' *British Journal of Psychology 83*, 1, 97–111.

Holmes, T.H. and Rahe, R.H. (1967) 'The Social Readjustment Rating Scale.' *Journal of Psychosomatic Research 11*, 213–218.

Holt, S. (2003) 'Child protection and men's abuse of women: An Irish study.' *Journal of Child and Family Social Work 8*, 1, 53–65.

Home Office (2010) 'British Crime Survey and other surveys.' Available at http://rds.homeoffice.gov.uk/rds/bcs1.html, accessed 8 September 2011.

Hotaling, G.T. and Sugarman, D.B. (1986) 'An analysis of risk markers in husband to wife violence: The current state of knowledge.' *Violence and Victims 1*, 101–124.

Humphreys, C. (2000) *Social Work, Domestic Violence and Child Protection.* Bristol: The Policy Press.

Jenkins, A. (1990) *Invitations to Responsibility: The Therapeutic Engagement of Men Who are Violent and Abusive.* Adelaide: Dulwich Centre Publications.

Johnson, M.P. (1995) 'Patriarchal terrorism and common couple violence: Two forms of violence against women.' *Journal of Marriage and the Family 57*, 2, 283–294.

Johnson, M.P. (2006) 'Conflict and control: Gender symmetry and asymmetry in domestic violence.' *Violence Against Women 12*, 11, 1003–1018.

Johnson, M.P (2008) *A Typology of Domestic Violence: Intimate Terrorism, Violent Resistance and Situational Couple Violence.* Boston, MA: Northeastern University Press.

Johnson, M.P. and Ferraro, K.J. (2000) 'Research on domestic violence in the 1990s: Making distinctions.' *Journal of Marriage and the Family 62*, 4, 948–963.

Johnson, M.P. and Leone, J.M. (2005) 'The differential effects of intimate terrorism and situational couple violence: Findings from the national violence against women survey.' *Journal of Family Issues 26*, 3, 322–349.

Kantor, G.K. and Straus, M.A. (1990) 'The "Drunken Bum" theory of wife beating.' In M.A. Straus and R.J. Gelles (eds) *Physical Violence in American Families.* New Brunswick, NJ: Transaction, pp.203–224.

Kaufman, J. and Ziegler, E. (1987) 'Do abused children become abusive parents?' *American Journal of Orthopsychiatry 57*, 2, 186–192.

Kelleher, P. and Associates with O'Connor, M. (1995) *Making the Links.* Dublin: Women's Aid.

Kelly, G.A. (1955) *The Psychology of Personal Constructs.* New York: Norton.

Kelly, G.A. (1963) *A Theory of Personality: The Psychology of Personal Constructs.* New York: Norton.

Kelly, L. (1988) *Surviving Sexual Violence.* Minneapolis, MN: University of Minnesota Press.

Kelly, L. (1995) 'Crisis Intervention Responses to Domestic Violence.' Paper presented at St George's Conference, London.

Kelly, L., Burton, S. and Regan, L. (1994) 'Researching women's lives or studying women's oppression? Reflections on what constitutes feminist research.' In M. Maynard and J. Purvis (eds) *Researching Women's Lives from a Feminist Perspective.* London: Taylor and Francis.

Kennedy, J. and O'Shaughnessy, M. (1998) 'Political conversations: Evolving team reflections.' *Feedback 8*, 1, 18–19.

Kewshaw, C., Budd, T., Kinshott, G., Mattison, J., Mayhew, P. and Myhill, A. (2000) *The 2000 British Crime Survey: England and Wales,* Home Office Statistical Bulletin 18/100. London: Home Office.

Khaw, L. and Hardesty, J.L. (2007) 'Theorizing the process of leaving: Turning points and trajectories in the stages of change.' *Family Relations 56*, 4, 413–425.

Kimmel, M. (2002) 'Gender symmetry in domestic violence.' *Violence Against Women 8*, 11, 1332–1363.

Kirkwood, C. (1993) *Leaving Abusive Partners.* London: Sage.

Kitzinger, C. (1993) 'Depoliticising the personal: A feminist slogan in feminist therapy.' *Women's Studies International Forum 16*, 5, 487–496.

Knox, J. (1558) *The First Blast of the Trumpet Against the Monstrous Regiment of Women.* available at www.swrb.com/newslett/actualNLs/firblast.htm, accessed 8 September 2011.

Kulkarni, S. (2007) 'Romance narrative, feminine ideals, and developmental detours for young mothers.' *Affilia 22*, 1, 9–22.

Lemert, C. (1992) 'Subjectivity's limit: The unsolved riddle of the standpoint.' *Sociological Theory 10*, 1, 63–72.

Leonard, K.E. (1999) 'Alcohol use and husband marital aggression among newlywed couples.' In X.B. Ariaga and S. Oskamp (eds) *Violence in Intimate Relationships.* Thousand Oaks, CA: Sage.

Leonard, K.E. and Quigley, B.M. (1999) 'Drinking and marital aggression in newlyweds: An event-based analysis of drinking and the occurrence of husband marital aggression.' *Journal of Studies on Alcoholism 60*, 537–545.

Letherby, G. (2003) *Feminist Research in Theory and Practice.* Buckingham: Open University Press.

Lundgren, E. (1995) *Feminist Theory and Violent Empiricism.* Aldershot: Avebury.

Luther, M. (1967, original 1531) *The Table Talk.* Translated and edited by T.G. Tappert. In *Luther's Works,* Vol. LIV, Philadelphia, 1967, p.8.

McCarthy, I.C. (1995) 'Women, poverty and systemic therapies.' In I.C. McCarthy (ed.) *Irish Family Studies: Selected Papers.* Dublin: Family Studies Centre.

McCarthy, I.C. (1997) 'Power, abuse discourses and women in poverty.' In S. Cobb (ed.) *Private Pain, Public Entertainment.* Special Issue of *Human Systems 8*, 239–249.

McCarthy, I.C. (2001) 'Fifth province re-versings: The social construction of women lone parents' inequality and poverty.' *Journal of Family Therapy 23*, 3, 252–277.

McGee, C. (2000) *Childhood Experiences of Domestic Violence.* London: Jessica Kingsley.

McKeown, K. and Kidd, P. (2003) *Men and Domestic Violence: What Research Tells Us.* Dublin: Department of Health and Children.

McLennan, G. (1995) 'Feminism, epistemology and postmodernism: Reflections on current ambivalence.' *Sociology 29*, 3, 391–409.

McNamee, S. (2004) 'Relational bridges between constructionism and constructivism.' In J.D. Raskin and S.K. Bridges (eds) *Studies in Meaning 2: Bridging the Personal and Social in Constructivist Psychology.* New York: Pace University Press, pp.37–50.

McWilliams, M. and McKiernan, J. (1993) *Bringing It Out in the Open: Domestic Violence in Northern Ireland.* Belfast: HMSO.

Mahoney, P., Williams, L.M. and West, C.M. (2001) 'Violence against women by intimate relationship partners.' In C.M. Renzetti, J.L. Edleson and R.K. Bergen (eds) *Sourcebook on Violence Against Women.* London: Sage.

Martin, S.L., Tsui, A.O., Maitra, K. and Marinshaw, R. (1999) 'Domestic violence in Northern India.' *American Journal of Epidemiology 150*, 4, p.417–426.

Maynard, M. (1994) 'Methods, practice and epistemology: The debate about feminism and research.' In M. Maynard and P. Purvis (eds) *Researching Women's Lives from a Feminist Perspective.* London: Taylor and Francis.

Millen, D. (1997) 'Some methodological and epistemological issues raised by doing feminist research on non-feminist women.' *Sociological Research Online 2*, 3. Available at www.socresonline.org.uk/2/3/3/.html, accessed 8 September 2011.

Miller, L. (2006) *Counselling Skills for Social Work.* London: Sage.

Mirrlees-Black, C. (1999) *Domestic Violence: Findings from a New British Crime Survey Self Completion Questionnaire.* London: HMSO.

Moe, A.M. (2007) 'Silenced voices and structured survival: Battered women's help seeking.' *Violence Against Women 13*, 7, 676–699.

Mooney, J. (2000) 'Revealing the hidden figure of domestic violence.' In J. Hanmer and C. Itzin (eds) *Home Truths About Domestic Violence: Feminist Influences on Policy and Practice.* London: Routledge.

Morgan, K. and Bjorkert, S.T. (2006) 'I'd rather you'd laid me on the floor and start kicking me: Understanding symbolic violence in everyday life.' *Women's Studies International Forum 29*, 5, 441–452.

Myerhoff, B. (1982) 'Life history among the elderly: Performance, visibility, and remembering.' In J.Ruby (ed.) *A Crack in the Mirror: Reflexive Perspective in Anthropology.* Philadelphia, PA: University of Pennsylvania Press.

Neimeyer, R.A. (1995a) 'An invitation to constructivist psychotherapies.' In R.A. Neimeyer and M.J. Mahoney (eds) *Constructivism and Psychotherapy.* Washington DC: American Psychological Association.

Neimeyer, R.A. (1995b) 'Constructivist psychotherapies: Features, foundations, and future directions.' In R.A. Neimeyer and M.J. Mahoney (eds) *Constructivism and Psychotherapy.* Washington DC: American Psychological Association.

Neimeyer, R.A. (1995c) 'The challenge of change.' In R.A. Neimeyer and M.J. Mahoney (eds) *Constructivism and Psychotherapy.* Washington DC: American Psychological Association.

Neimeyer, R.A. (1995d) 'Client generated narratives in psychotherapy.' In R.A. Neimeyer and M.J. Mahoney (eds) *Constructivism and Psychotherapy.* Washington DC: American Psychological Association.

Neimeyer, R.A. (1998) 'Social constructionism in the counselling context.' *Counselling Psychology Quarterly 11*, 2, 135–150.

Neimeyer, R.A. (2000a) *Meaning Reconstruction and the Meaning of Loss.* Washington DC: American Psychological Association.

Neimeyer, R.A. (2000b) *Lessons of Loss. A Guide to Coping.* Memphis TN: University of Memphis.

Neimeyer, R.A. and Levitt, H. (2001) 'Coping and coherence: A narrative perspective on resilience.' In C.R. Snyder (ed.) *Coping with Stress: Effective People and Processes.* Oxford: Oxford University Press.

Nelson, E. and Zimmerman, C. (1996) *Household Survey on Domestic Violence in Cambodia.* Phnom Penh: Cambodia Ministry of Women's Affairs, Project Against Violence.

O'Faolain, J. and L. Martines (1973) *Not in God's Image.* London: Temple Smith.

Ogrodnik, L. (ed.) (2006) *Family Violence in Canada: A Statistical Profile.* Ottawa: Statistics Canada.

Olesen, V.L. (2000) 'Feminisms and qualitative research at and into the Millennium.' In N. Denzin and Y. Lincoln (eds) *Handbook of Qualitative Research,* 2nd edn. London: Sage.

Parton, N. and O'Byrne, P. (2000) *Constructive Social Work: Towards a New Practice.* London: Macmillan.

Payne, M. (2007) 'Narrative therapy.' In W. Dryden (ed.) *Dryden's Handbook of Individual Therapy.* London: Sage.

Peled, E., Eisikovits, A., Enosh, G. and Winstok, Z. (2000) 'Choice and empowerment for women who stay: Toward a constructivist model.' *Social Work 45,* 1, 9–25.

Pence, E. and Paymar, M. (1993) *Education Groups for Men Who Batter: The Duluth Model.* New York: Springer.

Prochaska, J.O., Velicer, W.F., Rossi, J.S., *et al.* (1994) 'Stages of change and decisional balance for 12 problem behaviors.' *Health Psychology 13,* 1, 39–46.

Radford, J. (2003) 'Professionalising responses to domestic violence in the UK: Definitional difficulties.' *Community Safety Journal 2,* 1, 32–39.

Ramazanoglu, C. (1989) 'Improving on sociology: The problems of taking a feminist standpoint.' *Sociology 23,* 3, 427–442.

Raskin, J.D., Weihs, K.D. and Morano, L.A. (2005) 'Personal construct psychotherapy meets constructivism: Convergence, divergence, possibility.' In D. Winter and L. Viney (eds) *Personal Construct Psychotherapy.* London: Wiley.

Reinharz, S. (1992) *Feminist Research in Social Research.* Oxford: Oxford University Press.

Roche, S.E. and Wood, G.G. (2005) 'A narrative principle for feminist social work with survivors of male violence.' *Affilia 20,* 465–475.

Rousseau, J.-J. (1762) *Emile ou de l'Education,* edited by F and P. Richard, Paris, 1939.

Salamon, E. (1994) 'Who is a customer for social services: Some risks for abusive practices in the transition to purchaser – provider systems in Swedish social services.' In I.C. McCarthy (ed.) *Poverty and Social Exclusion.* In a special edition of *Human Systems 5,* 3/4, 305–318.

Saunders, D.G. (2002) 'Are physical assaults by wives and girlfriends a major social problem?' *Violence Against Women 8,* 12, 1424–1448.

Schröttle, M., Condon, S., Jaspard, M., *et al.* (2006) 'Comparative reanalysis of prevalence of violence against women and health impact data in Europe – obstacles and possible solutions. Testing a comparative approach on selected studies.' Available at www.cahrv.uni-osnabrueck.de/reddot/D_20_Comparative_reanalysis_of_prevalence_of_violence_pub.pdf, accessed on 8 September 2011.

Scott, J.C. (1985) *Weapons of the Weak: Everyday Forms of Peasant Resistance.* New Haven, CT: Yale University Press.

Shannon, G. (2003) *Child Law.* Dublin: Round Hall Sweet and Maxwell.

Somers, M. (1994) 'The narrative constitution of identity: A relational and network approach.' *Theory and Society 23,* 5, 605–649.

Stanko, E. (2000) 'The day to count: A snapshot of the impact of domestic violence in the UK.' *Criminal Justice 1,* 2.

Stanley, N. and Humphreys, C. (2006) 'Multi-agency and multi-disciplinary work: Barriers and opportunities.' In C. Humphreys and N. Stanley (eds) *Domestic Violence and Child Protection: Directions for Good Practice.* London: Jessica Kingsley Publishers.

Stark, E. (2007) *Coercive Control: How Men Entrap Women in Personal Life.* New York: Oxford University Press.

Steinmetz, S.K. (1977) *Cycle of Violence: Assertive, Aggressive and Abusive Family Interactions.* New York: Praeger.

Steinmetz, S.K. (1977/78) 'The Battered Husband Syndrome.' *Victimology: An International Journal 2*, 3–4, 499–509.

Stets, J.E. and Burke, P.J. (2000) 'Identity theory and social identity theory.' *Social Psychology Quarterly 63*, 3, 224–237.

Stets, J.E. and Straus, M.A. (1990) 'The marriage licence as a hitting licence.' In M.A. Straus and R.J. Gelles (eds) *Physical Violence in American Families.* London: Transaction Publishers.

Straus, M.A. (1977) 'Wife-beating: How common and why?' *Victimology 2*, 443–458.

Straus, M.A. (1980) 'Sociological perspective on the causes of family violence.' In M.G. Green (ed.) *Violence and the Family.* Boulder, CO: Westview.

Straus, M.A. (1990) 'Social stress and marital violence in a national sample of American families.' In M.A. Straus and R.J. Gelles (eds) *Physical Violence in American Families.* London: Transaction Publishers.

Straus, M.A., Gelles, R.J. and Steinmetz, S.K. (1980) *Behind Closed Doors: Violence in the American Family.* New York: DoubleDay.

Straus, M.A. and Gelles, R.J. (1990) *Physical Violence in American Families.* London: Transaction Publishers.

Strauss, A. and Corbin, J. (1990) *Basics of Qualitative Research: Grounded Theory Procedures and Techniques,* Newbury Park, CA: Sage.

Strauss, A.L. and Corbin, J. (1998) *Basics of Qualitative Research: Techniques and Procedures for Developing Grounded Theory.* Thousand Oaks, CA: Sage.

Stryker, S. (2002) *Symbolic Interactionism: A Social Structural Version.* Caldwell, NJ. Blackburn Press.

Swan, S.C. and Snow, D.L (2002) 'A typology of women's use of violence in intimate relationships.' *Violence Against Women 8*, 3, 286–319.

Swan, S.C. and Snow, D.L. (2006) 'The development of theory of women's use of violence in intimate relationships.' *Violence Against Women 12*, 11, 1026–1045.

Swan, S.C., Gambone, L.J., Sullivan, T.P. and Snow, D. (2008) 'A review of research on women's use of violence with male intimate partners.' *Violence and Victims 23*, 301–314.

Swan, V. (1999) 'Narrative, Foucault and feminism: Implications for therapeutic practice.' In I. Parker (ed.) *Deconstructing Psychotherapy.* London: Sage.

Taft, A., Hegarty, K. and Flood, M. (2001) 'Are men and women equally violent to intimate partners?' *Australian and New Zealand Journal of Public Health 25*, 6, 498–500.

Tamasese, K. (2007) 'Working for gender justice across cultures.' In A. Yuen and C. White (eds). *Conversations about Gender, Culture, Violence and Narrative Practice: Stories of Hope and Complexity from Women of Many Cultures.* Adelaide: Dulwich Centre Publications.

Testa, M., Quigley, B. M. and Leonard, K.E. (2003) 'Does alcohol make a difference? Within-participants comparison of incidents of partner violence.' *Journal of Interpersonal Violence 18*, 7, 735–743.

Tjaden, P. and Thoennes, N. (2000) 'Prevalence and consequences of male to female and female to male intimate partner violence as measured by the National Violence Against Women Survey.' *Violence Against Women 6*, 2, 142–161.

Todd, N. and Wade, A. (2003) 'Coming to terms with violence and resistance: From a language of effects to a language of responses.' In T. Strong and D. Pare (eds). *Furthering Talk: Advances in the Discursive Therapies.* New York: Kluwer Academic/Plenum Publishers.

United Nations (1995) *Beijing Declaration and Platform of Action, Domestic Violence Against Women,* Geneva: United Nations.

United Nations Population Fund (2000) *State of the World's Population*, available from www.unfpa.org/swp/2000/english/index.html, accessed on 8 September 2011.

United Nations Secretary General (2006) *Study on Violence Against Women. In-depth Study on all Forms of Violence Against Women.* Available at www.un.org/womenwatch/daw/vaw/violenceagainstwomenstudydoc.pdf, accessed 8 September 2011.

Vieraitis, L.M. and Williams, M.R. (2002) 'Assessing the impact of gender inequality on female homicide victimization across U.S. cities.' *Violence Against Women 8*, 1, 35–63.

Wade, A. (1997) 'Small acts of living: Everyday resistance to violence and other forms of oppression.' *Journal of Contemporary Family Therapy 19*, 1, 23–40.

Wade, A. (2000)' Resistance to Interpersonal Violence: Implications for the Practice of Therapy', unpublished doctoral dissertation. Victoria, BC: University of Victoria.

Wade, A. (2007) 'Despair, resistance, hope.' In C. Flaskas, I. McCarthy and J. Sheehan (eds) *Hope and Despair in Narrative and Family Therapy: Adversity, Forgiveness and Reconciliation.* Hove: Brunner-Routledge.

Walby, S. and Allen, J. (2004) *Domestic Violence, Sexual Assault and Stalking: Findings from the British Crime Survey.* London: Home Office Research, Development and Statistics Directorate.

Waldegrave, C. and Tamasese, K. (1994) 'Some central ideas in the "Just Therapy" approach.' *The Family Journal 2*, 2, 94–103.

Walker, L.E.A. (1979) *The Battered Woman.* New York: Harper and Row.

Walker, L.E.A. (1984) *The Battered Woman Syndrome.* New York: Springer.

Watson, D. and Parsons, S. (2005) *Domestic Abuse of Women and Men in Ireland.* Dublin: National Crime Council of Ireland.

White, M. (1989) *Selected Papers.* Adelaide: Dulwich Centre Publications.

White, M. (1995) *Re-Authoring Lives.* Adelaide: Dulwich Centre Publications.

White, M. (2000) *Reflections on Narrative Practice.* Adelaide: Dulwich Centre Publications.

White, M. (2007) *Maps of Narrative Practice.* New York: Norton and Company.

White, M. and Epston, D. (1990) *Narrative Ends to Therapeutic Means.* London: Norton and Company.

Whiteley, A. (2004) 'Grounded research: A modified grounded theory for the business setting.' *Qualitative Research Journal 4*, 1, 27–46.

Wilcox, P. (2006) *Surviving Domestic Violence: Gender, Poverty and Agency.* Basingstoke: Palgrave Macmillan.

Wood, J.T. (2001) 'The normalization of violence in heterosexual romantic relationships: Women's narratives of love and violence.' *Journal of Social and Personal Relationships 18*, 2, 239–261.

Wood, J.T. (2004) 'Monsters and victims: Male felons. Accounts of intimate partner violence.' *Journal of Social and Personal Relationships 21*, 5, 555–576.

Wood, G.G. and Roche, S.E. (2001) 'An emancipatory principle for social work with survivors of male violence.' *Affilia 16*, 1, 66–79.

Yllo, K.A. (1984) 'The status of women, marital equality, and violence against wives.' *Journal of Family Issues 5*, 3, 307–320.

Subject Index

Author Index